BEATING BURNOUT FINDING BALANCE

BEATING BURNOUT FINDING BALANCE

MINDFUL LESSONS FOR A MEANINGFUL LIFE

MELO CALARCO

WILEY

First published in 2023 by John Wiley & Sons Australia, Ltd

Level 4, 600 Bourke St, Melbourne, Victoria 3000, Australia

Typeset in Droid Serif 10pt/16pt

© John Wiley & Sons Australia, Ltd 2023

The moral rights of the author have been asserted

ISBN: 978-1-394-15459-3

 A catalogue record for this book is available from the National Library of Australia

Cover design by Wiley
Cover and chapter opener image: © marukopum/Shutterstock
Cover image: hiker: © SimpleB/Shutterstock

Disclaimer
The material in this publication is of the nature of general comment only, and does not represent professional advice. It is not intended to provide specific guidance for particular circumstances and it should not be relied on as the basis for any decision to take action or not take action on any matter which it covers. Readers should obtain professional advice where appropriate, before making any such decision. To the maximum extent permitted by law, the author and publisher disclaim all responsibility and liability to any person, arising directly or indirectly from any person taking or not taking action based on the information in this publication.

To my beautiful wife Kila, who is always there for me.

And to my dear daughters, Maalika and Alani, who mean the world to me. I hope the work that I do can help make the world you grow up in a more peaceful and beautiful place.

A special dedication to my 95 year old Dad,
who is the strongest and most resilient person I know.

CONTENTS

CONTENTS

ABOUT THE AUTHOR

Melo Calarco is passionate about three things: his family, travelling the world and helping as many people as possible live their best life.

As a certified mindfulness and performance coach, Melo has the unique ability to bring the best out of the people, and the companies, he works with. His results-based work is grounded in neuroscience, mindfulness, human behaviour, leadership training and other unique tools to help his clients find self-awareness, clarity, focus and, ultimately, success.

Melo learned to manage highly challenging and stressful situations, build mental endurance and rise above adversity from his life lessons on the road, where he cycled, trekked and travelled around the world on his mountain bike. He traversed Africa, Asia, India, Nepal, Europe and North America. Along the way, he had to overcome many obstacles and demanding encounters, including near-death experiences.

He now shares those deep experiences through his popular corporate programs, working with many global Fortune 500 companies, CEOs, directors, corporate executives and medical surgeons, as well as sporting professionals, Olympic athletes, actors, entrepreneurs, thought leaders and individuals who want to be the absolute best at their game.

Melo truly believes that everybody can live a life full of passion and potential without burning out and he is on a mission to empower as many people as possible to achieve this through his programs, workshops and one-on-one coaching.

His work has been described as truly transformational.

Melo loves spending time travelling with his family and exploring the Mornington Peninsula in Victoria, where he lives with his wife, daughters and beloved Swiss Shepherd, Koda.

INTRODUCTION

In my work as a mindfulness and high-performance coach, I have noticed a considerable increase in the rate of burnout over the past few years. I'm passionate about making a difference because burnout is continually on the rise globally, with the unrelenting pace of the modern world and the 2020 pandemic having made a significant impact.

Putting together a toolkit of preventative strategies to manage stress, build resilience and maintain wellbeing is far better than experiencing full burnout and then seeking the road to recovery. Regardless of whether you have experienced a partial or full burnout, are just feeling a bit tired and unmotivated, or if you are someone who is looking to make some improvements towards a more meaningful life, this book will give you the tools and techniques to reclaim balance and prevent the onset of burnout.

Over the years I have run many seminars, workshops and programs focusing on mindfulness concepts and various other techniques for preventing or overcoming burnout as well as helping high performers operate at their best. I am always touched and astounded by the feedback I receive weeks, months or even years later from participants sharing their stories on how the concepts and practices have helped them through difficult times, or saved their marriage, or even helped people negotiate serious illnesses.

When I hear individual stories from people I meet who have attended my workshops, I am reminded of why I love the work I do. It is these encounters that inspired me to write this book to help as many people as possible — including you.

My hope is that within these pages you will find inspirational stories, interesting concepts and some mindful practices and practical tips that you can easily implement to prevent burnout, find balance and live a healthy, meaningful life. My deepest aspiration is that you will adopt some of the simple techniques and incorporate them into your lifestyle to create a positive compounding effect, improve your overall wellbeing and find balance.

Furthermore, with the prevalence of burnout rising globally, I felt an innate need to support people through these challenging times. During the height of the 2020 pandemic, I supported more than 75 000 people globally through my corporate seminars and workshops, but I wanted to help further. I concluded that I not only *wanted* to write this book to support more people, but I *needed* to write it.

As the title suggests, this book will help you beat burnout and find balance in your life, but it will do much more than that. It will give you practical, implementable tools and techniques to prevent burnout, manage it or recover from it. You do not need to be experiencing burnout to benefit from this book. Each chapter also shares a valuable life lesson to help you operate at your best every day and to live your best life.

The book's three main takeaways, which I hope you will adopt, are:

○ the importance of self-awareness, self-regulation and self-care to prevent burnout

- o how to manage stress and overwhelm while thriving as a high performer

- o the benefit of living more mindfully and meaningfully.

I'd like to explain that this book does not outline in great detail what burnout is or its historical context; nor is it an in-depth analysis on mindfulness and the clinical research associated with it. There are many books that do this well. I prefer to spend time focusing on tangible ways of preventing burnout and introducing mindfulness into your daily life to find balance. It is one thing to learn about these concepts theoretically; it is another to actually practise them so you can feel the benefits for yourself.

Many of the stories I share on these pages are based on my personal experience and the lessons that I learned from cycling, trekking and travelling around the world on my mountain bike. I also capture some valuable lessons from other people I have worked with professionally over more than 25 years of working as a mindfulness and high-performance coach, including CEOs, corporate executives, medical surgeons, athletes and many other inspirational people from some of the world's leading companies. I interviewed close to 200 people from all walks of life while doing research for this book, and their unique insights and perspectives have been a valuable contribution.

Most of all, I want to share with you some of the techniques that I have tried and tested with many of my clients with positive results. The techniques are simple and easy to implement in your life so you can feel the benefits immediately. Some of these fundamental concepts and practices may already be familiar to you and this could be a gentle reminder that you need to take action.

How to use this book

Ideally, you should read this book chronologically, chapter by chapter, as each chapter has a particular underlying theme. I share stories, concepts, anecdotes, case studies and a life lesson in each chapter as well as short, practical mindful practices at the end of each chapter. The lessons and practices build on each other to give you a complete toolkit of self-coaching techniques and tips to help you navigate life with purpose and passion. For example, it makes sense to develop self-awareness (chapter 1) before self-regulation (chapter 4). But how you use the book also depends on your personal needs. You may choose to bounce through different chapters, depending on what you are looking for at the time.

The book contains some fantastic techniques and practices that can support you on your journey to living a mindful and meaningful life, but I do not propose that you adopt every single practice all at once. It is more beneficial if you grab one or two techniques that appeal to you personally and continue to practise them daily to experience the compounding benefits. My big goal is to simplify the complex and make the techniques easy to implement in your life, with very little effort, to create long-term, sustainable, healthy habits.

What I'd love is for you to pick up this book, learn a few techniques and implement them into your daily life so you, and everybody around you, can benefit. There is space for you to write on the pages, or you can download the worksheets and resources from **www.melocalarco.com**.

And what I'd love even more is to maybe one day bump into you on the street and listen while you share your story of how you benefitted from this book. ☺

With love and gratitude

Melo Calarco

CHAPTER 1

ON SELF-AWARENESS

The first step in preventing burnout and implementing any sustainable change in your life is developing your self-awareness. As you become increasingly self-aware, you will notice if you are working stressfully or feeling fatigued and you can take action to self-regulate depending on how you are feeling (you will read about self-regulation in chapter 4).

For this book, I interviewed close to 200 people who had experienced some sort of burnout and, alarmingly, 90 per cent of them said they were not aware they were burning out until it was too late. It wasn't until they had a panic attack or reached crisis point that they realised they were burnt out.

Put simply, *you can't change what you don't notice*. Developing self-awareness gives you the ability to practise self-control, to manage stress, to look at different perspectives, to have better decision-making skills and to create solutions. In this chapter we will explore the concept of self-awareness and how you can begin to cultivate a deeper understanding of your inner self, which will benefit many areas of your life. Let's start with a personal story on self-awareness and how it helped me to self-regulate in a very challenging situation.

Rural South Australia

One fine afternoon, five good friends and I sat around a coffee table and spawned the crazy idea of cycling around the world on our mountain bikes for a couple of years. As plans progressed, we looked at maps of Africa, India, Asia, Europe and the United States, and started roughly planning out some of the routes for circumnavigating the globe.

Over the next few weeks, for me the idea became ever more exciting, while admittedly also a little daunting. Unfortunately, my friends, one by one, slowly backed away from this absurd idea for

You can't change what you don't notice.

various reasons. And so, I was left with the choice of quitting and staying in my comfort zone, or going solo. Could I trust my self-awareness and intuition to make the right decision in this moment?

Despite family and friends trying to convince me otherwise, my decision was a resounding—and crazy—*Yes! Let's go for it!*

I started buying special lightweight camping equipment and kitting out my beloved bike with panniers (saddlebags) for the big adventure. I began doing training runs and exposing myself to different types of terrains and conditions.

I also became efficient in ways to carry and set up my equipment. After all, I needed to carry my bed, my kitchen, my wardrobe, my food, my water and myself on my bike on this big adventure. The training runs were sometimes difficult, but mostly fun as I got to push my boundaries and learn to negotiate different challenges. On one particular occasion, I was truly pushed to my limit and my self-awareness and ability to self-regulate were put to the test.

It was a long weekend in winter and there was a mild storm forecast for the remote areas of South Australia, where I lived at the time, so, as part of my training, I decided to head out on my mountain bike and go camping! According to the forecast, the storm didn't look too threatening—I didn't want to put myself in unnecessary danger—so I decided to give it a shot and headed out into fairly mild, wintry conditions. I was so excited to test out my new lightweight equipment and my expensive new tent.

Hour by hour, I cycled further and further away from home. By early afternoon, I noticed the storm clouds brewing on the horizon above the forest canopy and I could hear the gentle, percussive rumble of distant thunder. The landscape around me drew a stark contrast of vivid green forest pines with a looming sky of deep greys and dense, black rain clouds. I had never seen clouds like these in my life, and at that point, I wished I had my camera with me to capture this eerie moment (this was before mobile phones were an everyday accessory). Far away from any towns and deep in a forested area, I was feeling a mix of excitement, fear, strength and freedom. I thought it was probably time to start setting up camp as the dark clouds were continuing to change into obscure shapes and dusk was fast approaching.

I kept riding, but suddenly the mood changed entirely. The sky turned to black and visibility was getting very low. The deep, rumbling thunder was growing louder, and flashes of sheet lightning pierced the darkness. From out of nowhere, 100-kilometre winds started battering the environment and then, within seconds, the whole scene changed for the worse! Cold, stinging rain started belting across my body and I was instantly drenched from head to toe. The rain seemed to be coming at me horizontally as the wind pushed it hard against my frozen face. I didn't even have time to get my brand-new Gore-Tex rain jacket out. I was already wet to the bone from the rain.

It took all of my strength and focus just to keep my bike stable and negotiate the muddy path ahead. I glimpsed the path between the flashes of lightning as the thunderclaps grew stronger and more frequent. I kept riding and looked for a clearing to set up my tent, but I couldn't see much through the sheets of rain. Large tree branches and limbs started crashing all around me. And then, I couldn't believe my eyes: a fully grown gum tree was uprooted by the ferocious winds. I was officially scared and in danger.

I watched in fear and disbelief as large tree limbs were snapped effortlessly by the cyclonic winds and hurtled all around me. I had never seen anything like it and I learned later that it turned out to be one of the worst storms to hit Australia in decades — and I was in the middle of it!

I persevered a bit longer, trying to keep my bike upright against the relentless horizontal rain and wind. I was just about to stop when I heard an almighty crack behind me. It sounded like a shotgun. Suddenly, a falling tree struck me violently from the side, sending my bike and me crashing to the ground. It felt like a truck had hit me at full speed, knocking me to the ground and crushing the bike panniers carrying all my new equipment. I was in shock.

My leg was bleeding and my ribs felt crushed, but luckily I wasn't too badly injured, and I managed to get up. I wanted to make myself a shelter, but some of my tent poles were cracked and the tent shell was ripped. The horizontal rain continued, the howling winds grew even stronger, the temperature dropped rapidly and darkness truly set in. There was no way I could set up my damaged tent in these conditions so I tried to construct something with my bike and the ripped tent shell, but the wind was even too ferocious for that. There was absolutely no way I could light a fire with such intense wind and rain, and the flying branches and limbs were still crashing violently around me. I gathered all my belongings in a neat pile and managed to find a few biscuits in my bag, which I hurriedly ate to give myself some energy. By this time I was genuinely anxious as I was dodging falling branches and debris from above while I continued to look for shelter.

The world around me was literally crashing and crumbling. The wind was howling, branches were flying, trees were being uprooted, lightning was flashing, thunder was grumbling and I was officially in grave danger. I sat down beside my bike and piles of damaged equipment—cold, broken and drenched to the bone. I noticed my hands were frozen and bluish in colour, my teeth were chattering uncontrollably and my lips were numb as I felt hypothermia setting in. Crippled by fear and cold I did not know what to do!

My senses were heightened and I was very self-aware in this moment. Suddenly, a flash thought lit up my mind: *If the world around me is a chaotic mess, how about I look inside myself for some inner strength and solace? It's time to go within.*

In my pile of belongings, I found a small foil emergency blanket—you know those little square ones you think you will never use (because how could it possibly save anyone's life?). I gave it a try anyway. I wrapped it around my shoulders and hugged myself tightly with it. My next rational thought was to try some breathwork. My Tai chi master had taught me meditation and deep belly breathing techniques over the years, and I recalled him claiming these could help raise your core temperature as well as provide many other health benefits. So, I sat under my tiny foil blanket, put my hands on my lower belly and started to meditate. It took a while to settle and focus as I was constantly distracted by the wind howling through the treetops and the sounds of tree branches crashing around me. At times I was tempted to get up and run, but I had nowhere to run to, so I persevered with the breathing practice.

I diligently counted my breaths to stay focused on my lower belly area—1, 2, 3 ... 7 ... 59, 110, 210—and I counted into the high hundreds.

After a while, I started to feel warm, and actually even hot! It was beyond belief, but my thermal fleece was beginning to wick away the moisture from my core temperature, radiating outwards, and my clothes slowly started drying out. I continued counting, with my hands on my belly, and I felt myself drifting in and out of counting and consciousness for what seemed like a few hours. The storm was still crashing all around me, but I was starting to feel a sense of peace and security emerge from deep inside me, like a deep, still ocean beneath the raging waves above. I calmed down and started to believe that I was going to survive this. As I dived deeper inside myself, I felt myself drop down into another layer of subconsciousness as my meditation guided me deeper downwards and inwards. After some time, I actually felt a sense of total inner peace and stillness, oblivious to the outer world. I felt safe, I felt warm and I felt totally calm.

I am not really sure what happened to me over the next few hours. Time meant nothing. I was in a state of being that I had never experienced before. I can't explain it in words. I was not even sure if the storm was still raging around me because I no longer noticed the external world — only the world within me. It was timeless as I sat in this fine balance of a present state of awareness and deep, peaceful consciousness.

I must have sat in meditation from dusk until dawn, drifting between various brain states. I knew the worst was over when I heard the comforting sound of a solitary magpie starting its morning warble. I opened my eyes to see the first rays of sunlight penetrate the forest. It appeared that the storm had mostly passed. I noticed large tree limbs and debris strewn all around me. One particularly large branch was just a metre away, but I have no recollection of it crashing near me. My body was sore, and my legs had pins and needles as I tried to stand up. It took me a few attempts, but I finally managed to get up, feeling a little shaky and weary.

In the morning light, I got busy gathering my senses and my belongings, and temporarily fixing my bike enough to ride to safety. I managed to find a bit of food in my pannier to give me some renewed energy and began my journey home. Before I left, I took a moment to look around me in astonishment that I had just spent a whole night in this forest, all alone in the middle of a ferocious storm, without shelter. I could not believe that one minute I was hypothermic and scared to death and then, through the power of breath and meditation, I was able to self-regulate and feel totally safe, warm and secure.

With weary legs and a cold body I started pedalling on my journey back home to a warm house, a hot shower and some nourishing food. I processed my thoughts and reflected on my experience, grateful to be alive. I didn't tell any of my family and friends about this incident, partly because I was embarrassed and partly because they thought I was safe and sound in my brand-new tent.

You can influence your physiology by changing your psychology, and vice versa.

This challenging experience taught me one big lesson and it definitely changed my life in many ways. It taught me the power of self-awareness and 'going within' to self-regulate. It also taught me to trust that you will always have the resources inside you to deal with any situation, which served me well for the travelling adventures that followed.

To this day, I am still not exactly sure what happened between the many hours of dusk and dawn, but I do know this: I am now a firm believer in the profound potential of meditation and breathwork, and it has become my life's work personally and professionally. You can influence your physiology by changing your psychology, and vice versa. The power of the body and mind connection is infinite, and it all starts with self-awareness.

Life lesson: Self-awareness

Self-awareness precedes everything. When you develop self-awareness you become more mindful of your inner and outer environments. You can prevent burnout with awareness by realising what you are experiencing, assessing the situation and taking positive, decisive action in the moment.

Self-awareness: the first step

As I've already asserted, you can't change what you don't notice. It all starts with you, and developing strong self-awareness. A relationship with your inner world is the first step to preventing burnout and finding balance. If I was able to literally find calm in the eye of a storm through meditation and breathwork, I am sure these same techniques can help you remain calm in any challenging situation. You can always find peace within when you develop your deeper sense of awareness, and additionally your ability to self-regulate.

With self-awareness, you can reduce anxiety before it takes over. You can take a renewal break when you notice you are fatigued. You can manage external pressure and stress before you feel overwhelmed. It's a bit like driving your car and the oil light flashes on your dashboard. What happens if you ignore that sign? What happens if you keep driving for days on end without oil? The engine will simply burn out or blow up! It's the same with us. What happens if you notice you are feeling stressed or anxious, but you continually ignore the signs and just keep trying to push on through? You might get so many warning signs through your day—tight chest and shoulders, heart palpitations, lack of focus, fatigue, tension, poor sleep, and so on—but you just keep trying to push through. Unfortunately, there is a price to pay for this ongoing, unmanaged cumulative stress. The price is burnout.

As you read earlier, 90 per cent of the people I interviewed for this book stated they were not aware that they were experiencing burnout until it was too late. The other 10 per cent either ignored the signs or did not have the tools to deal with them. My aim is to give you practical tools and techniques that will help you read the signs and take proactive steps to prevent burnout in the first place—and developing self-awareness is the first step.

Emotional intelligence

In his bestselling book *Emotional Intelligence*, psychologist Daniel Goleman[1] describes self-awareness as the very first domain for developing emotional intelligence. When I'm running corporate leadership programs on this topic, I often ask the group the fundamental question, 'What is emotional intelligence?' I am met enthusiastically with some great responses, such as, 'being able to read the room', 'understanding other people's needs', getting along with your colleagues', 'having empathy towards your team members', 'listening to others', 'working together dynamically as a team', and so on. These are all accurate responses, but most people forget one fundamental aspect: it all starts with you! Self-awareness is the first step.

The two fundamental components of emotional intelligence are:

o *understanding yourself*: your goals, your values, your behaviours, your emotional responses and your thought patterns

o *understanding others:* their feelings, and sharing empathy and connection.

It's interesting how most people's answers include the second component and totally overlook the first, which is obviously the more important part. Knowing yourself first is paramount. How can you possibly interact with other people on a deeper level if you do not truly know yourself first? And I mean, truly know yourself deep down: know your behaviours, know your pain points, know your relationship with your emotions and know your tipping point. Know what you do when you feel stressed, sad, angry or upset. Do you recognise your behaviours? Do you withdraw? Do you become reactive? Do you blame others? All of this comes under the banner of self-awareness and sometimes your perception of yourself may be very different from the reality.

One of the general managers of a large bank that I work with explained to me how his team loved him so much and he was admired by them as a leader and a friend. He told me he stayed calm under pressure and never got angry at his team members during tough times. In the subsequent months, I began working with various members of his team and they told me the polar opposite: that he was manic, unapproachable, reactive and often moody. His perception of himself was totally different from how others perceived him. He obviously needed some training on self-awareness 101, which we did, and within months he improved dramatically. He became a much better leader, a better husband and a better person. The first step to good leadership and becoming a better person is self-awareness — and that comes from more introspection and reflection time.

The same is true for avoiding burnout and reclaiming balance in your life: the first step is self-awareness.

Why is self-awareness so important?

Practising self-awareness is all about learning to better understand why you feel the way you do and why you behave in a particular way. Developing self-awareness gives you the opportunity and freedom to change things about yourself, and the choice to respond in a certain way and ultimately to create the life you want. How can you possibly create the life you want when you don't know yourself deeply?

Being self-aware is about having a good knowledge and under–standing of yourself and being aware of your actions and behaviours. It's about knowing your strengths and limitations: knowing what gives you joy, knowing what creates an emotional response in you and what your basic needs are. Then, once you understand yourself better, you are better able to empathise, connect and communicate with others more personally and professionally. As a high performer, you are constantly working in demanding conditions and high-pressure situations where the ability to remain calm under duress is very important.

In terms of preventing burnout, the first step is to be aware of what is happening to your body and mind throughout the course of a day. Being acutely self-aware gives you the ability to make positive choices in various situations every day. It could be as simple as being aware of the choices you make, such as 'Should I stop for lunch, or not? Should I go to the gym tonight, or not? Should I stay back and work late, or not?' Burnout is something that can creep up on you over time when you are not making the right choices; therefore, being more aware of your choices and mindful of your basic self-care is very important. The constant wear and tear on the body and mind through lack of self-care and cumulative stress compounds over time and eventually wears you down.

> **Being acutely self-aware gives you the ability to make positive choices in various situations every day.**

Mindfulness 101

One of the best ways to develop self-awareness is to spend more time on your own and to adopt some mindfulness training and practices. I have been practising mindfulness and meditation for about 30 years and have seen the immense benefits in it. Throughout this book I will share various mindfulness stories, concepts, techniques and practices, and I sincerely hope you can benefit as much as I have.

At its most fundamental level, mindfulness is about paying attention to the present moment, without judgement, and being openly aware. It's about being present and engaged with where you are and what you are doing at the time. This sounds really easy in theory, but sometimes it is difficult to practise mindfulness in this busy, overstimulated world we live in. Sometimes we can overcomplicate the simple practice of mindfulness in the modern world and put so many convoluted terms to it that it seems confusing and difficult to achieve.

I like to keep it really simple and elegant: mindfulness is about being in the moment; it's about living your life with more presence and awareness. That's it!

During my travels, I stayed in a monastery in Vietnam, where life was all about living more mindfully everyday. The monastery shared the teachings of Thích Nhất Hạnh[2], a revered Vietnamese monk and Zen master who popularised the practices of mindfulness for several decades. The monastery was not a strictly silent retreat—unlike a Vipassana retreat, where you are not allowed to speak at all to anyone—but at this monastery you could only talk about the thing that you were doing at the time. For example, if you were chopping vegetables, you could only talk about the vegetables (like the beautiful orange colour of your carrot). If you were eating your meal, you could only talk about the aromas and flavours of your food. If you were washing the dishes, you could only talk about the dishes, the water temperature or the scent of the soap, and so on. You couldn't be washing the dishes while talking about the weather or eating your meal while talking about work. You had to be fully present with the task you were doing and only make conversation about it if you wanted to.

Paying full attention to the task you are doing at the time with all of your awareness and catching your mind when it drifts off sounds really simple. But I must admit, I found it quite difficult at first because it made me realise how not present I was when doing many of these everyday tasks, especially the mundane ones like washing the dishes. After some time though, I began to appreciate all of the things I did in my day more mindfully: everything from waking up, brushing my teeth, showering, cooking, eating, communicating, walking and even washing the dishes.

Mindfulness is not something new, and chances are you are practising it already, especially when you are engaged in things that you love doing. Think of a time when you were doing something you love and were fully immersed in that task with your full presence. This is mindfulness!

Formal and non-formal mindfulness practices

There are two main ways to practise mindfulness: formally and informally.

o *Formal practice.* This is when you physically stop what you are doing and do some sort of stillness practice. You might choose to close your eyes and pay attention to the sensations present in your body or rest your awareness on your breath and use it as an anchor to stay present. This could be practised for 90 seconds, five minutes, 10 minutes or longer. This is classically what you might consider to be a meditation practice, where you train your attention to stay in the present moment through your body and breath.

o *Non-formal practice.* This is about being more mindful of your daily activities and doing them with more presence and awareness (like I did while in the monastery in Vietnam). You think of all of the things you do in the day on autopilot, or in default mode, and you train yourself to pay more attention to them. The great thing about this is, it doesn't take any extra time in your day. For example, eating is something you do three to four times a day. You might eat on the run, or in front of the computer, or graze mindlessly throughout the day. However, when you eat more mindfully it's an opportunity to bring mindfulness to your day by simply paying attention to the flavours, aromas and taste of your food. Chances are, you will enjoy your food and the whole experience more.

These two practices are equally important as they mutually train your self-awareness and your ability to pay attention and focus on one task. For example, if you can't close your eyes and stay present with your breath for two minutes without your mind wandering, how can you stay focused at work for hours on end? Equally, if you can't stay fully present while you are having a shower for five minutes, how can you stay engaged doing the other 10 000 things that you do in a day. When we are more present and focused on the task at hand, we are at our best. A brilliant article called 'A wandering mind is an unhappy mind', by Killingsworth and Gilbert[3], contends that we are happiest when we are fully engaged in the task we are doing because our mind is able to stay present and not wander to unpleasant thoughts and feelings.

Killingsworth and Gilbert's research also states that 47 per cent of the time our mind is elsewhere—it's off task. That's nearly half of the time! The question is, where does it go when it wanders off? Does it ruminate in the past, or catastrophise about the future, or does it run wild thinking about a million things? This mind wandering can often be the cause of mild depression, overwhelm, anxiety and other mental health issues. One solution is to train your mind to be more present, more awake and more aware moment by moment. This will help you to develop a deeper self-awareness and enable you to stay focused on what is happening around you and within you.

Ask yourself what daily tasks you do on autopilot. Are you present when you're brushing your teeth, when you're having breakfast, when you're driving/commuting, when you're talking to someone, when you're listening? I'm sure there is some room for improvement for all of us.

Getting started

Now, it's one thing to talk about mindfulness in theory, but to actually experience the benefits we must implement the practices. Mind training is similar to physical training: you can read all the books you like about how to get physically fitter and stronger, but one day you actually have to do the exercise to gain the benefits. For example, if you want to run a marathon, you actually have to physically train over a period of months, not just read about it. It's the same with your mind: you actually have to do regular mindfulness training to feel the improvements.

I believe, to create this new habit in a sustainable way, you should start off with simple and short mindfulness practices, and then slowly build them up over time. Two of the simplest and easiest ways to get started in developing your self-awareness and ability to self-regulate are:

o a daily formal practice, like the 90-second
   breathing technique

o a non-formal practice, like mindful showering, mindful
   eating or mindful listening (or you can choose any of your
   daily activities).

You will find instructions on how to do these two practices at the end of this chapter, but here I would like to describe the profound effects of the 90-second breathing technique and when you can apply it.

The 90-second breathing technique

I have taught this practice to thousands of people over the years and many of them have given me amazing feedback on how it has helped them manage a challenging situation, get through a difficult task, relax before an important meeting, or manage their stress and anxiety.

One of the paramedics I coach was the first responder to a horrendous car accident in his neighbourhood. When he arrived on the scene, he recognised the car and started having a mild panic attack as he opened the car door and found his teenage son in the back seat. He froze for a moment in horror and did not know what to do. Then he remembered the 90-second breathing technique I had taught him. After doing the practice, he managed to calm down enough to recollect his thoughts and take action to save his son's life. He stayed calm throughout as he was aided by the other paramedics to bring his son safely to hospital, where he was treated for his wounds and eventually made a full recovery.

When we are in a stress response, the amygdala (a gland near the base of the brain responsible for the fight-and-flight response) fires up and hijacks our ability to make clear decisions and problem solve. However, when we breathe slowly and intentionally, even for just 90 seconds, we can down-regulate the overactive amygdala and initiate the relaxation response, so we can think more rationally and more clearly. We will discuss this in more detail in the following chapters, but for now let's get into doing some practice.

Can 90 seconds really make such a difference?

Please do not underestimate the short duration of this practice. I have seen the benefits time and time again and sometimes it even amazes me how profound the rewards are from such a short practice. The first great thing is you can always find 90 seconds in your day. A big barrier for people initiating a regular mindfulness practice is they believe they don't have the time. Secondly, the more you practise these 90-second breath breaks, the more you train your self-awareness and the ability to self-regulate. You achieve this by training yourself to slow down through your breath physiology, which in turn influences your psychology. Lastly, it doesn't matter whether you are an absolute beginner to mindfulness or someone who has a regular daily meditation practice, you can still reap the profound benefits from these short practices.

It's time to start the first step to preventing burnout by using two simple mindful practices to develop your self-awareness. Enjoy!

Self-awareness practices

Practice 1: 90-second breathing technique practice

The intention of this practice is to bring your full awareness to your breath and use it as an anchor to stay present.

Wherever you are, make yourself comfortable—whether that's standing, seated on a chair or lying down. Gently close your eyes, or half close them if you prefer, and rest your awareness on your breath. Relax your shoulders and rest your arms wherever is most comfortable.

When you are ready, take a deep, intentional breath into your nose, filling up your body with air (without force). Follow this with a slow, controlled exhale through the nose (and mouth) all of the way out, totally emptying your lungs. Feel a sense of new energy and vitality entering your body and mind with each in-breath and then feel a sense of release, or letting go, with each out-breath.

Continue gently inhaling and exhaling for about 10 rounds, or about 90 seconds, constantly working on making your breath slower, smoother and deeper. At the end of the practice, take your time to gently open your eyes and bring the calm awareness back into your day. You may want to set a timer on your device for 90 seconds.

Download a short audio version of this practice from **www.melocalarco.com**.

You can use this simple technique when you are feeling a bit stressed or overwhelmed, before a big meeting, when resetting between big projects or tasks, before bed and whenever you feel the need to. I recommend using this simple practice about four or five times a day. This will teach you to bring self-awareness and help you self-regulate within minutes. Please do not underestimate the short duration of the practice, as it is very powerful.

Practice 2: Mindfulness practice

This one is easy in theory. All you need to do is choose *one* thing you do every single day and give it your full attention. You may choose:

o Waking up	o Driving
o Eating	o Working
o Commuting	o Communicating
o Studying	o Bike riding
o Exercising	o Brushing your teeth
o Showering	o Cooking
o Walking	o Cleaning
o Listening	

The list is endless. Just choose *one* thing you normally do on autopilot and see what you can do to be more present while doing this task. Continue this practice for a minimum of 10 days. Chances are, the longer you do this, the more you will enjoy the task! Just remember, it is a form of attention training and will primarily help you develop your self-awareness.

CHAPTER 2

ON BURNOUT AND SELF-CARE

So, what is burnout anyway, and why is it affecting so many people in today's world? The World Health Organization (WHO) recently revised its definition of burnout for the eleventh time, changing it from a medical condition to a 'syndrome'[4]. While doing research for this book, I asked many people from various professions, 'What is burnout?' and I was surprised by the varied responses I received. In this chapter we will explore this question in more detail. We will look at ways to prevent burnout by initiating self-care practices so you can live a healthier and more balanced life.

The Southwest, United States

Although I have helped hundreds of people overcome or prevent burnout, to date I have not experienced a mental or emotional burnout myself. However, during my global adventure I was cycling through the Navajo tribal lands and I experienced a physical burnout, which took me some time to recover from.

I had been cycling long distances through the stunning scenery of the Southwest of the United States for a few weeks and camping alongside Navajo and Hopi Indians along the way. Most cycling days consisted of more than 200 kilometres in distance and I probably wasn't eating enough to fuel that amount of daily expenditure. It was an amazingly enriching experience as I spent time learning the ways of the indigenous people of this area and I also spent many hours alone with my thoughts as I traversed the vast desert plains of Arizona, Utah, New Mexico and Colorado. I even accomplished 10 push-ups in all four states at once. It's known as the 'four corners monument', where you can have a hand and a foot in each of those states at once and do a push-up.

One particular day on Highway 163, surrounded by the stunning backdrop of the majestic Monument Valley, my body said 'that's enough' and totally shut down. My legs cramped severely, my blood sugar levels dropped and I believe I had sunstroke. I vomited until I dry retched and I nearly passed out. I could barely stand up, let alone ride my bike any further. I had to stop. My body would not allow me to continue, so I set up camp on the side of the highway to get some rest. I literally collapsed in my tent and tried to rehydrate before I fell asleep from sheer exhaustion. I slept the rest of the day and through the whole night. When I awoke, I still felt weak and a little dizzy, but I ate breakfast to recoup some energy and decided I felt good enough to continue on.

As I was packing up my tent and getting ready to continue riding, I noticed many cars and buses stopping ahead of me, about 500 metres up the road. The passengers were getting out of their vehicles, taking some photos and continuing on their journey. When I finally managed to get back in the saddle and start riding again, I went to the location where everybody was stopping and it turned out to be the exact spot where Forrest Gump stopped running in the 1994 hit movie *Forrest Gump*, starring Tom Hanks[5]—an uncanny coincidence. I was just a few metres short!

It took me weeks to fully recover from that burnout, and I was extra careful not to let this happen again. I was mindful of my food intake and I was extra careful with my daily energy expenditure. Similarly to a mental or emotional burnout, had I listened to the signs earlier, I potentially could have avoided this physical burnout by staying hydrated and eating more high-energy snacks along the way, but I was too late in my response. This is often the case with burnout of any sort (mental or physical)—it's too late before we take action, and it can be prevented if we don't ignore the signs.

Melbourne, Australia

I was running the first session of a six-week mindfulness program for a leadership team in a large IT company with a cohort of about 15 people. The group was generally enjoying the content, participating well and showing interest in the mindfulness concepts. However, one of the team leaders, Pete—a sales executive—was sceptical. I usually welcome scepticism and part of my job as a facilitator is to break some of the myths and preconceptions and offer a new perspective.

However, Pete was different. He was exceptionally closed minded to the techniques. He stood up a few times during the session and said, 'I've got better things to do. I'm too busy. I have a team to manage and I should not be here. It's a waste of my time!' I acknowledged his statements and asked him to at least stick around for the rest of that particular session. Pete stayed against his will and continued to heckle and question the program for the next hour or so. I delivered the concepts to help him, and the rest of the group, with some techniques and practices for managing stress in their demanding roles as leaders.

During the session, I observed that above the table Pete was putting on a tough front with his strong words; however, under the table his legs were shaking uncontrollably throughout the session and he was quite nervous, fidgety and anxious in his mannerisms. I am quite familiar with recognising chronic stress and anxious behaviour as I have worked in mental health clinics and psychiatric hospitals for more than 15 years running programs for inpatients and outpatients. I genuinely felt sorry for Pete for having to put on a strong face in front of his peers while underneath he was quite fragile, anxious and weak, and I really wanted to help him as best I could.

At the end of the session, I thanked Pete for staying for the whole 90 minutes. I acknowledged his concerns and I invited him back the next week for the second session. Surprise, surprise, he did not return for session 2 or any subsequent sessions. I did try to reach out via email a few times, but there was no response.

Months passed and I thought about Pete a few times while I was delivering more programs to the same company, hoping that he would join one of the sessions and I could support him, but I didn't see him there again.

A few months later I was running a four-week program at a psychiatric clinic when guess who walked in the door? That's right, Pete—the same guy who had heckled me and refused to stay in training because it was a waste of his time. I could tell from his appearance and slow gait that Pete was fully burnt out. He was barely comprehensible and was in the clinic to get help regaining his mental health. With empathy, I welcomed him into the group. I did not mention our previous acquaintance—in fact, I'm not sure he recognised me. He sat in the front row looking down at his paper and pen. To open the session, I collectively asked the group the question, 'Who plans to stay for the whole four weeks?' Pete was the first to put up his hand as he shyly said, 'Oh yes, yes, yes, I have to. I need to get better.'

I only wish Pete had persevered during the initial program at his company because he potentially could have learned some tools and techniques to self-regulate and equip him to manage stress better. I did my absolute best to help Pete and he did attend the complete four-week program. He participated in the discussions and exercises and at the conclusion of the program he told me he found the mindfulness practices 'pretty good', and that they were really helping him.

Pete is a perfect example of an overstimulated high achiever working in a stressful environment to meet overwhelming demands to the detriment of his own physical and mental health. The constant wear and tear of chronic stress on his body and mind eventually led him to a full burnout. Unfortunately, Pete is not alone. In the course of a year in my coaching business I meet many Petes—fortunately some are in the early stage of pre-burnout, but most reach out only after experiencing a full burnout.

Life lesson: Burnout

The self-care practices that keep you healthy and balanced are the same ones that lead to burnout when neglected. Through self-awareness and improving your self-care you can be more attuned to your body's needs and more proactive towards your health and wellbeing.

So what is burnout?

As I touched on early in the chapter, the WHO recently redefined the classification of burnout from a medical condition to a 'syndrome'. Burnout is now defined by International Classification of Diseases (ICD-11) as follows:

> Burn-out is a syndrome conceptualized as resulting from chronic workplace stress that has not been successfully managed. It is characterized by three dimensions:
>
> o   feelings of energy depletion or exhaustion
>
> o   increased mental distance from one's job, or feelings of negativism or cynicism related to one's job; and
>
> o   reduced professional efficacy.[6]

Busy professionals in high-pressure jobs are most at risk—people such as medical professionals, first responders, lawyers, business executives, social workers, teachers, principals and so on. In fact, no-one is exempt from burnout, especially in the fast-paced, overstimulated environment that we are all exposed to. We live in a world where we are always 'on'; we are always accessible and have trouble switching off from work so it's becoming more difficult to find balance.

According to the 2022 ELMO Employee Sentiment Index, nearly half (46 per cent) of Australians are feeling burnt out[7], while in 2021 the American Psychological Association reported that 79 per cent of employees had experienced work-related stress, including lack of interest, motivation or energy. Meanwhile, a 2022 poll from Microsoft found 48 per cent of employees and 53 per cent of managers globally reported feeling burned out at work[8].

The global COVID-19 pandemic also contributed greatly to the increasing incidences of burnout. In Australia alone, more than 52 per cent of employees admitted taking time off work due to pandemic lockdowns[9]. I had many calls from CEOs, general managers and C-suite executives who usually wouldn't reach out to me admitting they were struggling, feeling anxious and uncertain, and questioning their capacity to keep going. Many struggled with the constant lockdown restrictions and others were feeling stressed, exhausted and felt like they were approaching burnout. In addition, many companies reached out to me for assistance in supporting their employees' mental health. At the height of the pandemic, I was supporting more than 75 000 people globally in virtual seminars and workshops in a large variety of workplaces.

Statistics aside, we don't need to look too far to find many of our peers are showing signs of fatigue, exhaustion, energy depletion, lack of motivation, disengagement and anxiety, and you may be experiencing some of these feelings yourself. We don't suddenly come out of a global pandemic that affected so many people's mental health and wellbeing and miraculously return to 'business as usual'. The world as we know it has changed; burnout is on the rise and we need to adapt to the ever-changing conditions. It's normal to feel tired sometimes, or to feel exhausted after completing a big project or after a big day at work, but it's not normal to feel like this for a prolonged period of time.

During my interviews for this book, which included people from diverse roles and industries, I discovered some common themes and causes for the way they were feeling. One common factor was the gradual onset of burnout, which could extend over weeks, months and years without people recognising the signs until it was too late. The main signs and symptoms spanned across three main areas—physical, emotional and behavioural—as depicted in figure 2.1 (overleaf).

Physical	Emotional	Behavioural
◦ Feeling drained	◦ Feeling undervalued	◦ Social isolation
◦ Frequent headaches or migraines	◦ Lack of self-worth	◦ Withdrawal from responsibilities
◦ Tight jaw, neck and shoulders	◦ Feeling trapped	◦ More absenteeism
◦ General aches and pains	◦ Unmotivated	◦ Being late for work
◦ Low immunity	◦ Cynical and negative	◦ Procrastination
◦ Often sick	◦ Lacking purpose and direction	◦ Avoiding difficult tasks
◦ Change in appetite	◦ Detached and disengaged	◦ More errors
◦ Poor sleep patterns	◦ Feeling defeated and lonely	◦ Lack mental clarity
◦ Tired often	◦ Emotional eating	◦ Reactive outbursts
		◦ Frequent drug and alcohol use to cope

Figure 2.1 types of feelings

Real-life examples of burnout

One of my clients, a managing director of a large real-estate firm, described burnout as an unrelenting weight on her shoulders all of the time. She had no appetite, and no desire or energy to do anything fun. She couldn't sleep and had a niggling, underlying feeling of anxiety all day long. On top of her demanding workload and pressure at work she had three young children under 10 years of age and the younger two had special needs. She was exhausted most of the time, doing absolutely nothing for herself, not exercising, feeding her children better than herself and she rarely slept more than three hours a night. She knew she was experiencing stress but did not know what to do about it. Then burnout snuck up on her over a period of two years without her noticing it. As she put it, she disregarded the signs and it took her more than 12 months to recover.

A busy general practitioner I worked with suffered severe burnout after running multiple medical clinics and not looking after himself. He joked to me that the advice he was giving to his patients was the exact same advice he was blatantly ignoring for himself. He got to the point where he had to stop working momentarily and take time to restore his mental health and wellbeing. After some extended leave and reclaiming some healthy habits, he was able to make a full recovery and is approaching his work in a different way now. He takes some afternoons off and incorporates regular exercise and meditation into his daily routine.

One of the most interesting definitions a client shared with me was that he described it as 'burn-in' first and 'burnout' second. By this he meant that externally he could keep going with his role and obligations and manage his stress to a certain degree, but internally he lost his sense of purpose and direction. He worked in a large, multinational company for nearly three decades and due to a variety of changes that happened within the organisation, he no longer felt valued or appreciated for the hard work he was doing. He persevered for two more years with low levels of engagement and motivation until he experienced the full mental and physical symptoms of burnout and the only solution for him was to remove himself from that environment by resigning. For nearly three decades his work had been his identity and at first, he had trouble finding a sense of purpose outside of that, but now he has found hobbies and interests and is spending more time with his family.

Stages of burnout

It is always difficult to give a definitive model for the stages of burnout because it can be a totally different experience for each person, and it fluctuates continually through various stages. However, based on my research and the conversations I have had with many people I have worked with, burnout usually (but not always) takes form in some of the following stages:

○ *Stage 1:* You have a strong drive to work hard and prove your worth, so you work relentlessly hard to achieve this.

○ *Stage 2:* You prioritise your work above everything else and you start letting go of your basic self-care practices.

○ *Stage 3:* You continue meeting your high workload demands and ignore all other areas of life; e.g. family time, social life, hobbies, health and fitness.

○ *Stage 4:* Either you notice the signs but ignore them, or you keep pushing through and are 'disconnected' from your feelings.

○ *Stage 5:* You feel empty, and lack direction and purpose. You may fill the emptiness with alcohol, substances or bad habits.

○ *Stage 6:* This further progresses to poor mental health and feelings of depression or anxiety.

○ *Stage 7:* You may experience panic attacks or reach a crisis point with some sort of breakdown, and then have a mental, physical and emotional burnout.

All of this can be managed or prevented the quicker we become aware of it. As we saw in chapter 1, the more we become self-aware, the quicker we can avoid these stages progressing into a full burnout.

Nobody is exempt from burnout

Burnout can affect anyone, regardless of their status and intelligence—from top-ranking athletes like Australian Open winner Ash Barty, to celebrities like Arianna Huffington, some of the highest achievers in the world can experience burnout. One of the smartest people academically that I have come across in my coaching practice is a cardiovascular surgeon and associate professor who lectures in medical robotics and medical research around the globe. At first, I asked myself, how can I possibly help somebody so smart? However, I soon learned that it was a case of increasing his basic self-care habits and teaching him some simple mindfulness self-regulation techniques. His overactive mind was getting the better of him and he just couldn't switch off. He was running a busy medical practice and struggling to find a work–life balance.

He was at the middle stages of burnout when I met him, but he did not want to admit it. Luckily, his wife saw the signs and recommended he get help to prevent a full burnout. My point here is that although he is extremely intelligent and, being a doctor, knows the health consequences of not looking after yourself, he struggled to maintain his own self-care practices. Being a clinician, he was a little sceptical at first about the mindfulness and breathing techniques, but he is now practising the techniques daily and is back on track to finding balance in his life. He is also now an advocate for mindfulness and breathwork, which he shares with his patients, his family and friends, and, as he says, 'anybody who will listen'.

A too-busy world

Sadly, I have countless examples of other high performers who work in stressful environments and have forgotten about their own self-care, especially when the work pressure and demands get high. It sometimes amazes me how ironic it is that the things we need the most to be high performers and work well through challenging situations are the very things that we stop doing when work gets busy—for example, the basics of exercise, nutrition and sleep.

It's ironic and counterintuitive that when you're feeling overwhelmed and stressed you might say things like:

o   I'm too busy to exercise today.

o   I'll skip the gym tonight. I've got too much to do.

o   I've got too many meetings to stop for lunch (or you mindlessly eat in front of the computer).

o   I'll just grab takeaway tonight. I'm too tired to cook.

o   I'm too busy to have a sick day.

And the list goes on. Does this sound familiar?

We really need to change our counterintuitive mindset because what we need most to stay energised through the tough and busy periods of work and life is regular exercise, good food, adequate rest and a good night's sleep.

The good news about beating burnout

Although the causes of burnout can be rather complex, the prevention and recovery can be more straightforward. Firstly, if the WHO defines burnout as 'resulting from chronic workplace stress that has not been successfully managed', then the first step is to be more proactive towards managing your stress on a daily basis. Secondly, if burnout is a consequence of cumulatively not looking after yourself, then I'd like to offer a simple and implementable solution by reversing the equation and increasing your daily self-care practices.

Put simply:

Cumulative lack of self-care = poor health and burnout

Cumulative increase in self-care = optimal health and balance.

I know it's not rocket science, but I do know, from working with thousands of clients over the years, that we all know that basic self-care is common sense, but unfortunately it's not always common practice. There are some wonderful books available that discuss the importance of these self-care habits in more depth: whole books on exercise, detailed books on nutrition and others on sleep, meditation, stress management and wellbeing. You probably have some on your bookshelf. These are all great resources and they give valuable advice, but you actually have to take action and implement the learnings to reap the benefits. My goal with this book is to distil the complex and give you accessible, implementable information and techniques that you can easily incorporate in your life to prevent burnout and find balance again.

Self-care essentials

To beat the cumulative impact of burnout, you need to start by looking after your fundamental physical and mental health first. I know it's sometimes easier said than done, but let's take a look at some of the foundational pillars of self-care for staying physically and mentally energised. I'm not going to go into great detail here because I'm sure you know the benefits of these basic self-care practices already.

The fundamental pillars for staying physically and mentally energised are:

- *Physical*
  - regular exercise
  - healthy nutrition
  - adequate sleep

○ *Mental*

- renewal breaks

- regular meditation (or downtime)

- mental stimulation outside of work.

Often when I present these fundamental pillars in my workshops it is common for people to tell me that while these are great reminders, they know this stuff already. However, my hope is that they are more than great reminders and that you can start reclaiming some of these well-needed habits, because they are imperative to preventing chronic stress and, ultimately, burnout. I have seen on many occasions that reclaiming these simple self-care habits can make a world of difference to people's daily energy levels, mental clarity and focus as well as the ability to manage daily stressors better. The less-desired option is to experience a full burnout first and then slowly start including these self-care habits as part of your rehabilitation and recovery. I know which option I would take!

I invite you to ask yourself these questions every single day:

'What have I done for *me* today?' and

'What have I done that's just for me, that makes me feel good, that gives me joy, that fills up my cup?'

Whether it's exercise, eating a nutritious meal, practising meditation, going for a walk, listening to music, being with family, chatting with friends or anything that nourishes you, make sure you do something just for yourself every single day. As simple as this sounds, it is the first step to beating burnout and finding balance in your life again. It's so important to prioritise your physical and mental health before it's too late because nobody else will. It's time to look after *you* first, so that you can be more energised, perform better, be more present, stay calm under pressure and enjoy life more fully.

Let's look more closely at reclaiming some of these fundamental self-care habits.

Exercise

We all know we need regular activity, and we all know how good we feel after we exercise. In terms of physical health, it's essential for weight management, cardiovascular health, muscle development and so much more. The benefits of exercise are well publicised in terms of boosting your mental health because they are great for stress relief and also for elevating your mood through the release of endorphins.

Here's a question for you: What can you do daily to prioritise your exercise, whether it's a brisk morning walk or a jog, a yoga or Pilates class, going to the gym, a boxing class or anything that gets the body moving? Aim for something that you can easily fit into your day.

Nutrition

Essentially, food is fuel for your body and brain, and you need good, clean fuel every day. Now the thing is, there are so many differing and confusing perspectives on what constitutes a healthy diet that I'm not even going to attempt to summarise them here, but I'm sure you know what's good and not good for you. Whether it's having a healthy breakfast, not skipping lunch, eating more regularly, portion control, healthy smoothies, more fruits and vegetables, more vitamins and minerals or simply drinking more water.

Maybe it's having less caffeine and fewer sugary snacks to keep you going and having some fruit, nuts and healthy snacks on hand instead. It may be to have better weekly meal preparation, so you don't reach for that quick takeaway when you are too tired or time poor to cook. Perhaps it's simply eating more mindfully, away from the computer, and having a proper lunch break to renew your energy. Aim to make one simple improvement to your daily diet and you will feel the benefits immediately. What can you improve about your daily eating habits?

Adequate sleep

Let's face it, sleep is the fundamental pillar that governs everything else related to your mental and physical wellbeing. Poor sleep leads to low energy the next day, mental fog, bad food choices or cravings for sweet/salty foods, an inability to focus, low mood and poor functionality. We all know how good we feel when we get a good night's sleep of about eight hours! We are energised, we have mental clarity and focus, better problem-solving capacity and decision-making skills, and we can cope with the demands of a big day at work or in life generally.

Many busy executives tell me that they can get by on about five hours' sleep. The key term I hear is 'get by'! Do you want to just get by, or would you like to thrive under pressure, have better cognition and achieve more every day with less stress? The key is a good night's sleep. We will discuss this in more detail in following chapters, but the best tip I can give you here is to create a tiered approach to winding down. Close your workday, turn off devices at a certain time each night and create at least a two-hour window before bed where you wind down—for example, dim the lights, have a hot tea, have a bath, read a book or do anything that you associate with winding down.

Regular renewal breaks

We are not machines. We cannot keep going 24 hours a day, seven days a week without any consequences. Most people don't give themselves regular renewal breaks throughout the day; they just keep pushing through all day and all week, which only results in fatigue at the end of their workday and exhaustion by the end of the week. We can only work in peak performance mode for around two hours at a time before our attention wanes, we lose focus and clarity, and our cognitive ability is compromised. Most people do not give themselves permission to stop and they keep working through fatigue, but I guarantee, if you stop for 10 minutes (or so) to renew your energy, your next two hours will be more productive. Regular renewal breaks are a necessity in terms of managing your daily energy levels and avoiding burnout. What can you do to punctuate your day with regular renewal breaks?

Mental stimulation outside of work

Most of the busy executives and professionals I work with don't make time to keep up their hobbies and interests. The more senior they get, the less time they have that is not consumed by their work. This may not sound too important, but having more interests outside of work will help you manage stress at work, and when you are engaged in your hobbies you are able to switch off from work. Mental stimulation outside of your work is great for your mental health; it helps you be more resilient to stress and helps you find balance. Whether it's learning a musical instrument, learning a language, playing sports, fishing, cooking, drawing or anything else you enjoy, what can you do to reclaim some hobbies or try something new?

Mindful meditation or downtime

I can talk forever about the benefits of meditation and I will share more in the coming chapters, but here I encourage you to try some mindful meditation to help you reclaim balance in your life, even if it's just 10 minutes a day. I also understand meditation is not for everyone: just getting some downtime in your day where you are not plugged into a device or computer is equally beneficial. For example, going out for a short walk, a bike ride, sitting at the beach or just sitting on a bench in a park—anything that gives you some mental space to calm your mind. What can you do each day to switch off and find some downtime?

* * *

Now the thing is, if I ask you to go away and do these six things in the coming weeks, chances are you will do them for a little while, but you may not continue with all of them and will slowly slip back to your old ways. It's all too much to try to include in your already busy week.

Commence by adding one healthy ritual to your life and once it becomes established into a daily habit you can anchor other habits to it.

So, in the activity at the end of this chapter, I will ask you to choose *just one* self-care habit that you feel you need to reclaim that will give you the most benefit in your life right now. Choose one and make it into a goal that you can implement this week and that you can measure. For example, if you choose exercise, instead of saying, 'I will exercise more this week' (this is not measurable), you could say, 'I will walk for 20 minutes each day before or after work', or 'I will go to the gym three times a week', or 'I will walk 10 000 steps a day'. Something that is measurable and achievable.

There are three things I do every morning that set me up for a good day so that I can be at my best. I start the day with a brisk morning walk at around sunrise, so I get that boost of serotonin to wake me up, followed by a short meditation practice to set some positive intentions and find some mental clarity. Then I have a healthy breakfast to fuel my body and brain for the day ahead. Three wins before the workday has even started that make me feel energised. I call these my 'non-negotiables' and slot everything else around them. I didn't start with all three though. I started with just the walk and thought to myself, *Since I'm walking every morning, I may as well do my meditation practice immediately afterwards.* Then, after some months, I added the healthy breakfast. This is called 'habit anchoring' or 'habit stacking'. Commence by adding one healthy ritual to your life and once it becomes established into a daily habit you can anchor other habits to it.

Furthermore, when it comes to starting a new goal, the first step is often the hardest, so I like to make the first step *impossible for you not to achieve in the next seven days.* Read that again! For example, if your goal is to walk every morning before work, perhaps the first step is to put your sports shoes and clothes by your bedside the night before, or maybe it's to buy a new pair of sports shoes. Make it impossible for you not to achieve.

Good luck on your first step. Jump into the activity box at the end of this chapter and choose your one daily self-care habit.

More good news

Rebecca was in the same six-week mindfulness program as Pete. She was fairly quiet in the group. She wrote lots of notes and politely participated in all of the practices, but she did not offer much during group discussions. She seemed a little tired and a bit sad. I was beginning to wonder whether she was getting much out of the sessions, but at the end of the six weeks her feedback survey was surprisingly positive.

Almost a year after I completed that program, I bumped into Rebecca at a city café during her lunch break and I invited her to join me for a coffee. She seemed positively energetic and much sprightlier than I remembered her. As we chatted, she said she really wanted to thank me for those sessions because they changed her life. She explained that she diligently kept up the daily self-care practices and referred to the notes she took during the sessions to practise the mindfulness techniques. She started by walking every morning before work instead of checking her emails; eating healthier; and meditating almost every night before bed (and consequently having a good night's sleep). These small changes translated into more energy and engagement at work, more presence and connection with her family and much less stress. She further explained that a year earlier, during my coaching sessions, she was having marriage problems, she was experiencing depression, and she couldn't see a way out of her stressful, busy life.

I asked her what caused the big change. She pondered pensively for a moment and said, 'There wasn't a big one. There were lots of small, incremental changes that lifted me up.' She explained that when she initiated her daily self-care, along with the mindfulness training, it progressively made her feel more energised and self-aware, which led to an upward trajectory in her life. Everything fell into place and she started enjoying her work more; her relationship with her husband and children improved; and she even took up a new hobby: playing guitar! Hearing that made my day and consolidated that small, incremental changes can have a profound long-term impact.

The good news is that burnout can be avoided if we read the signs and are proactive towards our health. There is no reason it should sneak up on us if we are mindful with our self-care practices. Let's get to work and take that first positive step towards beating burnout and finding balance!

Burnout-busting practice

As we saw in this chapter, reclaiming some of your fundamental self-care habits can provide profound benefits for improving your physical and mental wellbeing. We are going to reclaim your physical and mental energy in three easy steps.

Step 1

Write a few points in each column saying what you can start doing.

Physical energy	Mental energy
What can I do on a daily basis to increase my physical activity? (e.g. morning/evening walk, gym, exercise class)	*How can I incorporate regular short renewal breaks in my day so I'm not exhausted every night? (e.g. tea break, quick walk, eat away from computer)*
Healthy nutrition	**Hobbies and interests**
What simple improvement can I make to my daily eating habits? (e.g. meal regularity, more healthy snacks, less sugar, less alcohol)	*What can I do weekly to stimulate my mind with something outside of work? (e.g. learn an instrument, sports, cooking, fishing, hiking)*

Adequate sleep	Regular meditation (or downtime)
How can I improve the quality of my sleep by creating healthy sleep association rituals? (e.g. exercise throughout the day, digital switch-off time, wind-down rituals)	*How can I ensure I practise a short, mindful meditation practice or give myself some downtime every day? (e.g. meditation app, breath practice, take some time out)*

Step 2

Circle *only one* of the following habits and make a commitment to include this in your daily self-care habits:

- ○ regular exercise
- ○ healthy nutrition
- ○ adequate sleep
- ○ renewal breaks
- ○ regular meditation (or downtime)
- ○ mental stimulation outside of work.

Step 3

Turn your circled habit into a measurable goal and write three steps you can follow to achieve this goal. For example, if your goal is to increase exercise, instead of writing 'exercise more', write something like, 'Walk every morning for 20 minutes'. And remember: your first step must be impossible for you not to achieve in the next seven days.

1 _____

2 _____

3 _____

Bonus step

Once this habit becomes established, you can anchor or stack the other habits on top.

Note: Not enough space? Download a free accompanying workbook from **www.melocalarco.com**.

CHAPTER 3

ON STRESS AND RESILIENCE

Stress is a very broad topic. We know we need a certain amount of stress to drive us and motivate us towards our goals, but how much is too much? What is the fight-or-flight response and how can it help or hinder us? In this chapter I will share a story about fight-or-flight and discuss the mechanisms behind a stress response. I will also look at the evolution from stress to burnout and ways to manage and prevent this.

Virunga National Parc, Rwanda

Suddenly the jungle foliage in front of me started shaking violently. I heard a thunderous primal groan and out of nowhere, a massive 600-kilogram silverback gorilla came charging straight towards me! At this moment I learned the true meaning of the fight-or-flight response. Not the textbook meaning that I learned in high-school biology or the work–stress version we are all familiar with, but the true primitive meaning of the terms 'fight', 'flight' and 'freeze'!

In less than a microsecond I felt my whole body being fuelled by adrenaline. I felt my skin chill, my muscles get ready to run, my stomach contract and my eyes on full alert ready to take action. Should I fight, flee or freeze? I froze! I was paralysed by shock and fear and my whole body stood tensely.

I took a breath and let out a big sigh. Once I was over the initial shock, I remembered what François, our mountain guide, had said to us in the briefing before we set out in search of the elusive mountain gorillas of Rwanda. He said if any of them mock charge you, or walk towards you, just stop in your tracks and do not make any eye contact with them whatsoever. I trusted François's guidance as he had worked for many years with Dian Fossey from the famous *Gorillas in the Mist* movie[10]. The mountain gorillas of Virunga were his family.

So there I was, looking down at my mud-sodden boots, feeling a mix of fear and excitement surging through my body as the muscular silverback brushed directly past me and kept on walking. He stopped a few metres ahead of me, sat on his backside, effortlessly ripped up some lush foliage and started chewing on it.

I hesitantly lifted my eyes up from the ground and, against François's advice, glanced into his striking eyes. Then something really strange happened. I witnessed this majestic peaceful being in front of me and my fear instantly dissipated. Although his large stature and muscular body were intimidating, his human-like eyes and face were soft and kind. In that instance, I felt the connective nature of all things, man and animal. I felt love, compassion and kindness, and closely connected to this stunning beast.

I felt the full spectrum of primal emotions, ranging from fight, flight, freeze, fear and excitement, to love, connection, peace and harmony. I felt part of the ecosystem they call 'life on earth' as we spent the following hours with this male silverback's lovely family. I was honoured to witness the interactions of this mountain gorilla family in all of its splendour. I also noticed that all of the stinging pain I had on my bleeding legs from trudging through dense, stinging foliage and thorny bushes had totally disappeared.

Among the group of about 12 gorillas, there were foraging mothers, doting aunties, cheeky teenagers and even a gorgeous six-month-old toddler with soft black curls being carried by its mother, all under the watchful eye of the large silverback male. Somehow, in the thicket of the dense jungle, one of the curious teenage male gorillas managed to steal a guide's machete and was wielding it around like an uncoordinated young boy. This caused some dangerous fun and frivolity between the guides and the cheeky teenager primates but luckily nobody was hurt. The more time we spent together immersed in this unique encounter, the more human-like their expressions and mannerisms became as I sat in awe of their presence.

After some time immersed in this unique jungle interaction, I experienced the polar opposite of the fight-or-flight response when the young baby gorilla clambered off its mother's back and started wobbling its way directly towards me like a fragile little child. It crawled and clambered until it was about a metre away. Then it raised its arms as if it wanted me to pick it up. Obviously, we were not allowed to touch the gorillas, but I was so close that it would have been difficult to back off quickly without tripping over the tangled jungle floor beneath my feet. It was centimetres away from me as I felt a surge of oxytocin and serotonin (relaxation response) and what I would describe as pure, blissful joy! My body totally relaxed, my heart felt warm and my smile of pure joy was so big it hurt my face. This moment in time touched me deeply and the image of this baby gorilla with arms outstretched is etched in my heart and mind forever.

Moments later it started raining heavily and the caring mother scooped up her baby and headed through a small hole into a bamboo thicket, disappearing into the dense bamboo foliage. One by one the rest of the family slowly filed in after her and to my utter surprise, we were motioned by the guides to follow them inside. Here we all were, humans and gorillas, huddled metres away from each other, sheltering collectively from the torrential rain. The tangle of bamboo foliage was so dense we could not stand up. Just like the gorillas, we humans were forced to manoeuvre on all fours in the restricted environment while the gorilla family foraged and happily chewed bamboo shoots around us. It was so dark in the dense thicket that it was hard to tell the difference between humans and gorillas. It was exhilarating being so close to these wonderful beings.

All at once I sensed a sudden change of mood as François and his guides started communicating nervously. I noticed one of our friendly machine-gun-carrying guides dive further into the thicket and seek deeper refuge. Something wasn't right. We were trying to understand what was happening when we heard violent crashing and pounding outside our concealed place. It sounded like a bulldozer crashing through the jungle foliage around us. François started letting out some deep, guttural groans, which were the same deep, primal sounds he had made earlier as we were heading up the mountain in search of the gorillas. He had previously explained that this is the sound the guides make to let the gorilla family know that we are here and that we are friends. It is the same deep, guttural sound that gorillas make within their family groups.

François continued letting out these primal groans, which comforted me somewhat as we could hear the crashing of foliage getting closer and closer to us. With military precision, François signalled to all of us not to move a muscle and to stay exactly where we were. *Here I go again: fight, flight or freeze*, I thought. I felt a mix of sensations flooding through my body again: from excitement, to fear, to joy, to shock, to elation and everything in between.

There before us, just outside our bamboo thicket entrance, blocking out all of the remaining daylight, stood a huge black figure. Was the silverback coming inside? This gorilla was even bigger than the male silverback. It was the second silverback male of the family. He must have been over 700 kilograms in weight and, apparently, he had been following us covertly the whole time. François continued his deep, groaning calls, calming the situation as we sat motionless, trapped in our restricted environment. The huge figure entered the shelter, stopped for a moment scoping the mix of humans and gorillas, and then swiftly demonstrated a mock charge, giving my Icelandic travelling companion, Hilmar, a backhander on his shoulder on the way through.

Although I was petrified and expecting much worse, I could see that after his mock charge he meant no harm and that he was just showing us who was the boss. My initial surge of cortisol and adrenaline started to subside as he also settled inside the bamboo shelter watching over his extended family as we all waited out the rain together. I noticed I had been holding my breath in fearful anticipation the whole time, so I let out a long, sighing breath. I felt somewhat exhausted from these two significant fight-or-flight experiences all in the space of two hours, but I also felt high and energised from the unique experience. I have never felt more alive—when your senses are on super high alert and in real-life danger, you feel completely alive and alert.

This unique experience taught me that the primitive fight-or-flight response is real and deeply ingrained in our genetic make-up, which has helped us survive as a species for thousands of years. I learned that it is only designed for short-term stimulus, to get us out of that situation, and that we then need mechanisms to switch it off. I also discovered the polar opposite response, being the relaxation response, when I felt safe and connected to these amazing animals. This memory is etched in my body and mind forever.

Life lesson: Stress and resilience

The stress response is only designed for short-term stimulus, which is helpful in a threatening or challenging situation. However, to maintain balance, we need to learn to deactivate it when it's not needed and initiate the relaxation response more regularly.

Modern-day fight-or-flight (the stress response)

The primitive fight-or-flight response is a handy mechanism. It has helped humans survive and evolve into what we are today. While our modern-day threats or stressors are not likely to be the primitive sabre-tooth tigers or silverback gorillas in the wild, they may be in the form of your boss, your workload, looming deadlines, financial pressures, conflicting priorities and much more. Many people activate this stress response frequently in a day—it can even stay with them for a whole day or week. This leads to overload on the body's physiology and overstimulation of the nervous system, resulting in poor health. We need to learn methods for deactivating this stress response before it affects our long-term health.

Our bodies cannot differentiate between a real threat and a perceived threat.

The mechanisms that take place in a real life-threatening fight-or-flight response are the exact same ones that the body undergoes during a perceived threat or under extreme stress. Our bodies cannot differentiate between a real threat and a perceived threat. For example, you might be tossing and turning in bed, stressed about something at work, triggering a fight-or-flight response at 2 o'clock in the morning with stress chemicals pumping through your body even though you are lying under your warm blanket, safe from any harm. You have manifested the stressor in your mind and initiated the stress response.

This constant over-activation of the fight-or-flight response is damaging to the body and the mind and can cause a gradual burnout. We need methods to disrupt this stress response and the associated physiology before it creates long-term damaging effects. One of the best methods you have learned already is the 90-second breath technique described in chapter 1, which is very powerful in deactivating the stress response and nipping stress in the bud before it overwhelms you. There is another breathing technique—deep diaphragm breathing—that is also very effective for managing chronic stress, and I'll share this with you later in this chapter.

Achieving balance

Let's dive a bit deeper into the neuroscience of what goes on in the brain when it is operating in chronic stress mode most of the time. When we are constantly under stress, the amygdala, which is a small gland in the primitive part of the brain, raises the general alarm to initiate the stress response. Here's what happens in the brain and body within a micro-second of a threat: the body prepares for action as certain brain regions fire up; then the hypothalamus and primitive amygdala signal the body to turbo-charge into full alert in preparation for a threat, be it real or perceived. The pituitary gland and thyroid gland kick into gear and raise the metabolic rate, sending out messages to secrete stress hormones and chemicals. This activates the sympathetic nervous system (SNS) and the adrenal cortical system (ACS) to flood the body with about 30 different chemicals and hormones, including adrenaline, noradrenaline and cortisol. This in turn prepares the body for the threat: should I run (flight), should I turn around and prepare to fight, or should I freeze?

At the same time, the non-essential physiological processes that we don't need in this moment slow down or switch off. These include our digestion, higher thought processes, immune system and sexual function (we're not really thinking of this when we're being chased by a tiger).

Then, in a matter of seconds, the body is on high alert:

- *The pupils dilate* to let in as much light and information as possible.

- *Saliva decreases* as the digestive system shuts down (some people experience this when speaking publicly).

- *The heart rate and blood pressure increase*, diverting a flood of blood to the muscles to prepare to sprint or take on an attack.

- *The skin chills* as the veins send blood away from the skin layer to the major muscle groups, getting ready for action. This reaction can give you 'goose bumps' as the hairs stand on end, increasing sensitivity in the body.

- *The major muscle groups contract* as the blood glucose and adrenalin levels rapidly increase in preparation for action.

- *The lung bronchioles dilate*, taking in more oxygen and infusing the body with oxygen for a burst of emergency action.

- *The liver works extra hard* to convert glycogen for quick, readily available fuel.

- *The spleen contracts*, pumping out white blood cells and platelets in preparation for a physical injury.

- ○ *The stomach constricts,* diverting blood elsewhere for energy.

- ○ *The whole body and brain* are in a state of high alert.

And all of this happens in a matter of seconds. *This is full fight-or-flight mode!*

As you can imagine, this is resource heavy for the body's systems and is not designed to be switched on all of the time. It is only designed for short-term activation, to help you get through a situation. Constant activation of this stress response will overload the sympathetic nervous system, and your chronic stress may lead to what is called 'allostatic load' or 'allostatic stress'. This is when the body's systems are slowly breaking down from the constant wear and tear of chronic stress on the body and mind. We are not machines. We cannot function at full speed 24 hours a day, seven days a week without any consequences.

I had a corporate client who thought he could. He owned multiple global businesses that were very successful, and he worked across three different time zones: Australia, the UK and Asia. He would jokingly boast of his all-nighters and the fact he only got about 10 hours' sleep in a week. He would work constantly at his many offices worldwide, at airport lounges, on aeroplanes and wherever he could open his laptop. He rarely exercised, ate poorly and at irregular times, did not take breaks, slept minimally, and was on high alert all the time. He wore his busy-ness as a badge of honour and was proud of his ability to work around the clock without stopping.

Eventually, his body said *Enough!* and his digestive organs started shutting down. His endocrine system was shot, his body stopped producing testosterone and other fundamental hormones and chemicals, his blood pressure went through the roof and he was in a serious health crisis. He was hospitalised for weeks with drips and tubes in every orifice and he was fully burnt out, physically, mentally and emotionally. This is probably the worst case of burnout I have seen. Fortunately, over time he made a slow recovery and, needless to say, we started working on his basic self-care, which we made non-negotiable. It took nearly two years and he has now made a full recovery, eats regularly, meditates daily, sleeps much better and works hard—and he takes regular renewal breaks every day. He still runs multiple businesses, but in a more sustainable way. He was lucky because he got a second chance at life—but not everybody does.

In short, the more you initiate the stress response and do not have the capacity to switch off or self-regulate, the more prone you are to chronic health problems like heart disease, hypertension, diabetes and neurological disorders. You are also likely to suffer chronic anxiety, depression and other mental health problems. As we have seen, the first step to managing stress is self-awareness: reading the signs and noticing the 'oil light' when it comes on. The second step is training yourself in how to self-regulate and to be able to deactivate the stress response and initiate the polar opposite physiological response, which is known as the relaxation response.

The relaxation response

If the stress response is often referred to as the 'fight-or-flight response', then the relaxation response—which allows your body to rest, digest and rejuvenate—could be referred to as the 'rest, heal and digest' response. I know which one I'd rather be spending more time in! When we are in the stress response, the sympathetic nervous system dominates, and when we are in the relaxation response, parasympathetic activity dominates. Homeostasis (or balance) is found when we can learn to balance these two autonomic branches—in other words, 'switch on' when we need to and 'switch off' when we can (see figure 3.1).

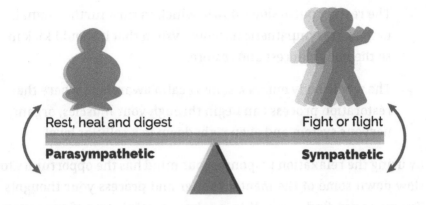

Figure 3.1 creating balance in your day

One of the best ways to initiate the relaxation response is to practise breathwork or mindful meditation. The relaxation response looks something like this:

○ The eyes totally relax and may even close when there is no possible threat present.

○ The saliva increases as the digestive system wakes up and begins gentle metabolism in the body.

> **One of the best ways to initiate the relaxation response is to practise breathwork or mindful meditation.**

○ The digestive organs and liver, spleen and pancreas begin their normal recuperative and restorative function.

○ The heart rate and blood pressure decrease as there is no need for any vigorous activity associated with fight-or-flight.

○ The chest and lung area relaxes as your breath slows down and you breathe deeper into your lower belly or diaphragm area; this also allows more oxygenated blood to get to the brain and the rest of the body.

○ The resting pulse slows down, which in turn further signals to the parasympathetic nervous system that it should kick in so the body can rest and restore.

○ The whole body enters a state of calm awareness where the restoration process can begin through your muscles, organs, nervous system and even right down to a cellular level.

By using the relaxation response, your mind has the opportunity to slow down some of the mental chatter and process your thoughts. You may even find yourself in a calm, peaceful state of awareness where thoughts may come and go gently, without judgement. You can start finding more balance in your life by initiating the relaxation response more frequently.

The amygdala hijack

In an ideal world, to find homeostasis in your life, you would fluctuate fluidly between the sympathetic and parasympathetic states. You might have periods of intense work in the sympathetic nervous system where you are thinking, planning or problem solving for a few hours and then you take a short break—maybe a 90-second breath break or a walk around the block—to activate the parasympathetic nervous system so that you rest and recover. Then you might go into another period of focused work, and so on. Most of us don't spend enough time in the rest, heal and digest phase and just keep trying to push through without any breaks, maybe relying on caffeine, sugar or stimulants to keep going.

One of the problems in the modern world is that we don't give ourselves permission to stop. We are always switched on and feel the need to work continuously at an unrelenting pace to get everything done. I encourage you to give yourself permission to take a short break to rest and reset, because if you stop for five or 10 minutes, your next two hours will be far more productive. If you keep trying to push through without any breaks, your cognitive function declines and your mental performance is compromised.

Cognitive functions take place in the front part of the brain, known as the pre-frontal cortex, but unfortunately, if you are not taking adequate breaks you constantly initiate the stress response and the amygdala (at the back of the brain) kicks in to hijack your attention. This amygdala hijack takes over your pre-frontal cortex, which not only reduces your performance, but also keeps you in a stress response—eventually leading to chronic stress (see figure 3.2).

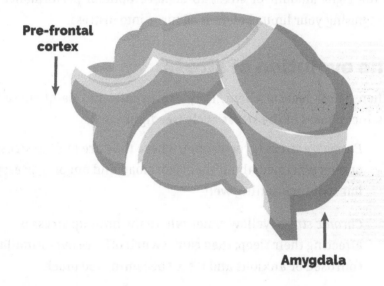

Pre-frontal cortex

Amygdala

Figure 3.2 amygdala hijack
Source: Brain image: © NotionPic/Shutterstock

Think for a moment about all of the cognitive faculties and skills you need at work or in life, such as planning, problem solving, decision making, analytical thinking and having mental stamina. These get weaker when you work under constant stress, while your amygdala and stress response get stronger and stronger. It's like training your muscles: the more you train a body part, the stronger it gets. It's up to you to determine which part of the brain you would like to train: the prefrontal cortex (or thinking part of the brain)—by initiating the relaxation response more often—or the primitive amygdala—by working under stress for long periods.

Now don't get me wrong, we actually need a certain amount of stress—such as deadlines, a big project or anything that pushes us to an objective outcome—to drive us, motivate us and help us achieve our goals. The right amount of stress is good for us; it's only when it tips over the balance that it turns to distress and you start feeling fatigued, anxious, unmotivated and exhausted. It's all about finding the balance of the right amount of stress to achieve optimal performance and recognising your limits before it all turns into distress.

The evolution of stress

When I first meet a client, they are usually in one of these four distinct phases of the stress cycle (see figure 3.3):

o   *Everyday stress* (green zone), where they are feeling stressed or overwhelmed about their workload and ongoing pressure but still functioning well

o   *Chronic stress* (yellow zone), where the built-up stress is affecting their sleep; they can't switch off, are overstimulated, confused or anxious and it's all becoming too much

o   *Allostatic stress* (orange zone), where they are starting to feel worn out, unmotivated, exhausted and can't concentrate; normal tasks are more difficult and they have low energy

o   *Burnout or poor mental health* (red zone), where they are no longer able to function cognitively; their mental health is compromised and is negatively impacting many aspects of their life.

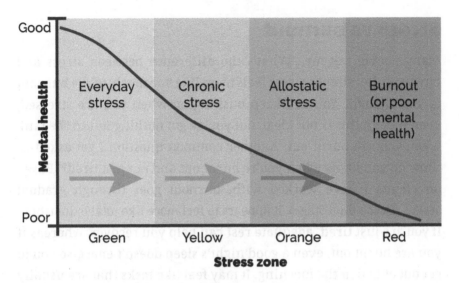

Figure 3.3 four phases of the stress cycle

Obviously, the earlier on in the stress cycle you take action, the easier it is to regain your physical vitality and mental energy. The closer you are to allostatic stress, or burnout, the more effort you'll need to get back to being balanced and functioning well again. The lesson here is: don't wait until it's too late or more difficult (orange or red zone). Take action in the early stages (green and yellow zones) to prevent the progression of stress to burnout. In the early stages, it may be as simple as increasing your self-care practices and learning a few easy techniques to manage your daily stress, while it requires much more effort in the latter stages.

I met Sandra, a busy HR professional, in the early stages of chronic stress, and it did not take long to establish some healthy habits again. We introduced a simple daily meditation practice and in a matter of weeks she was back to her full, energetic self again. Compare this to Mark, a busy executive who had experienced panic attacks and a full burnout before seeking help. He had to take time off work and it took him months instead of weeks to recover.

Stress vs burnout

Many people ask me, 'What's the difference between stress and burnout?' Put simply, stress feels more like 'too much' while burnout is 'not enough'. You can keep pushing on when you are stressed, even though this is not ideal, but you've got nothing left in the tank when you are burnt out. Another common question I get asked is, 'How do you know when you're burnt out and not just tired?' Based on clients I have worked with, burnout goes through gradual stages. In the final stages, it appears to feel more like total exhaustion. If you are just tired, adequate rest can help you recover, whereas if you are burnt out, even a good night's sleep doesn't energise you to get out of bed in the morning. It may feel like tasks that are usually easy for you are becoming very difficult, and you may find it harder to stay positive and engaged at work and at home.

A few words on resilience

Developing resilience is important to enable us to manage overwhelming experiences.

Resilience is often described as the ability to bounce back from tough situations or life events; to adapt, dust yourself off and keep moving forward with composure. It is also about having the awareness to stay measured and calm in stressful or challenging times or during traumatic experiences.

I interviewed many people about resilience while doing research for this book and heard some interesting analogies. The most unique and humorous story about staying calm in the face of adversity came from an Australian soldier who was on duty in Iraq in 2005. He was in Baghdad on morning sentry duty on the second floor of an old concrete building. The area was classified as a 'green zone', meaning it was a fairly stable and low-risk environment. He had made his habitual morning plunger coffee and had left the coffee cup in the makeshift kitchen while he went to the provisional rest room. He was sitting on the toilet with his rifle beside him when there was an almighty explosion on the floor below him, sending him hurling across the room. It turned out to be a suicide bomber with a truck full of 7 tonnes of explosives. Once the dust had settled from the explosion, in shock and disbelief, the soldier noticed a toilet roll had landed next to him, so he calmly picked it up to clean himself up, got dressed and cautiously walked through the rubble and falling debris back to the kitchen. Miraculously, his coffee cup was still sitting there, untouched by the explosion. He picked it up, took a sip, dusted himself off and went back to his post.

Developing resilience is important to enable us to manage overwhelming experiences. It helps us to maintain balance during difficult or stressful periods in life. The resilience of soldiers is a great example of how to remain calm and poised under extreme pressure, as this story demonstrates. We all get knocked down from time to time and it's up to us to choose how we dust ourselves off and get back up again. One of my favourite Japanese proverbs of all time is 'Fall down seven, stand up eight'. It's not about how you get knocked down—it's about how you continue to get back up again.

The power of the breath

As we saw in previous chapters, the breath is one of the most powerful tools for deactivating stress, and a great way to initiate the relaxation response. One of the best techniques for rebalancing the nervous system in periods of high stress is through intentional, deeper and slower breathing practices with a focus around the lower belly area. This is often known as deep diaphragm breathing. I learned this technique about 30 years ago while immersing myself in internal martial arts, and I can honestly say that it is my favourite 'go to' exercise any time I'm feeling stressed or overwhelmed.

I believe in this technique so much I have continued to practise a form of diaphragm breathing every single day and I continue to see the many health benefits.

With normal ribcage breathing, which is predominantly shallow in nature, the diaphragm (the parachute-shaped muscle just below the lungs) is only pulled down 1 to 2 centimetres. In contrast, diaphragmatic breathing encourages the diaphragm to be pulled down 4 to 10 centimetres. What does this mean? For every centimetre of diaphragm pulled down during breathing in, the volume of air in the lungs is increased by about 300 cc. There are countless benefits to this kind of breathing, including more oxygenated blood to the body and brain, increased mental alertness, massage of the internal organs, a regulated nervous system and increased immune system function. Aside from these great physiological benefits, it also helps to bring you back to the present moment and to deal with any situation with full presence of mind.

International keynote speaker Emma Seppälä gave a powerful TEDx Talk titled 'Breathing happiness'[11] in which she highlights the power of the breath. She describes the incredible story of Jake, a marine corps officer in Afghanistan, who was in the last vehicle of a military convoy that was blown up by an IED (improvised explosive device). Jake looked down in shock to see both of his legs severely damaged below his knees. In that moment, he remembered a breathing technique he had read about in the book *On Combat* by Lieutenant Colonel Dave Grossman where he teaches a technique commonly called 'box breathing'. Box breathing involves breathing in for a count of four, holding for a count of four, exhaling for a count of four and holding for another count of four. Thanks to this breathing technique, Jake was able to remain calm and have presence of mind. With this presence of mind he was able to check that his men were okay, give orders to call for help and tourniquet his own blown-up legs before passing out. He later found out that if he had not had that presence of mind he would have fallen into a coma or bled to death. Exercising the breathing technique saved his life.

Diaphragm breathing and the box breathing technique have very similar physiological effects. Taking control of your breath physiology helps you to take some control of your mind. Diaphragm breathing helps to stimulate the vagus nerve, which in turn activates the relaxation response, curbing feelings of stress or anxiety and regulating the mind. Once you focus all of your attention and awareness on your deep belly breathing, you can start feeling more centred and grounded because you use your breath to anchor yourself into the present moment. I regularly share this technique with many of my overstimulated clients, especially those with symptoms of anxiety and those who have trouble sleeping. Once they learn to shift their awareness from their head down to their body (using diaphragm breathing) they automatically calm down and become less anxious.

Better quality sleep: a bonus of deep breathing

How would you like a better night's sleep?

This is a question I often ask at my corporate seminars. Alarmingly, at least 85 per cent of the room raise their hand immediately—sometimes even 100 per cent. I then go on to share this diaphragm breathing technique in the workshop and encourage them to practise it at home. For example, if you wake up at about 2 am and start overthinking or creating anxious thoughts, simply lie on your back, place your hands on your belly area and follow your breath in and out of your body a few times. As you breathe in, your belly expands and as you breathe out, your belly naturally sinks and contracts. All of your awareness goes down to your body (out of your thoughts) and you gently slow the rhythm of your breathing down, which associates your mind with deep rest and sleep. It may take a few rounds of breath, say 10 or more, and it is a practice that gets better the more you do it as you improve your ability to self-regulate. The feedback I have received from some of the busy executives I work with is 'Best sleep I have had for years' and 'That's the first time I have slept all the way through—eight hours straight' and 'Oh my God, I woke up feeling so energised this morning—had the deepest sleep ever!'

When I'm teaching this technique to a corporate group, or one-on-one with a client, they often fall asleep. There are usually a few snorers in the room and they are shocked when they suddenly wake up a few minutes later with their colleagues staring at them. Recently, I was amused when I did an early evening virtual coaching session with a surgeon via Zoom and he fell into such a deep sleep during the meditation that I couldn't wake him up at the end of the session. So I went upstairs, had dinner with my family, came back down and he was still asleep. I went back up, put the kids to bed and then went back down to check on him and found him shuffling himself awake. He was a little embarrassed and shocked that nearly two hours had passed!

Falling asleep during meditation or deep breathwork is quite common and it's usually a sign that you are exhausted and not getting enough sleep or renewal breaks during the day. In this fast-paced and overstimulated world we live in and with our 'always on' mentality, insomnia is fast becoming a growing global problem, with as many as 50 to 60 per cent of people suffering[12]. The good news is, once you practise diaphragm breathing regularly, you can use it as an effective tool to self-regulate before going to bed or if you wake up during the night.

When to use deep breathing

Most people only seek deep breathing techniques as a way of trying to overcome stress—in other words, they only use it when they are feeling totally stressed or anxious. This is very beneficial, but I recommend also using it when you are feeling okay because the more you do it, the better you train yourself to initiate the relaxation response so that you use it preventatively instead of reactively. The 90-second breath break you learned in chapter 1 is a great way to interrupt a stress response and deactivate the amygdala, while deep diaphragm breathing is effective for creating a deeper calm within yourself. You can use the diaphragm breathing technique upon awakening to energise yourself, before bed to calm down, at work to renew your energy, in a meeting to stay focused, at traffic lights to stay calm, while waiting in a queue to remain patient, on the train to unwind—anywhere and anytime.

One of my best client success stories is that of a professional singer I worked with who suffered periods of exhaustion mixed with high anxiety. She was approaching burnout stage. Luckily, she had been taught diaphragm breathing by her singing coach many years earlier so she was able to tap into it quite quickly to feel the benefits.

It only took a matter of weeks to transform her from someone who was highly anxious and could not sleep more than three hours a night, to someone who slept eight hours a night. As a result, her anxiety all but disappeared and her mental health improved dramatically. She was very diligent with her breathing homework. Her singing coach had taught her a very valuable technique that she probably didn't value so much at the time, but I was quite pleased that I was able to help her complete her recovery journey.

I could keep talking forever about the many benefits of diaphragm breathing and there are so many great articles and books outlining the therapeutic benefits of breathwork. But, as I keep saying, you actually have to do the practices to feel the benefits for yourself.

Stress and resilience practices

Practice 1: Deep diaphragm breathing

The intention of this practice is to strengthen your ability to self-regulate when you are feeling stressed, overwhelmed or anxious, or during any challenging situations. You can also use it any other time to reap the benefits of fresh, oxygenated blood to the body and brain.

Wherever you are, make yourself comfortable—whether that's standing, seated on a chair or lying down. This is a good practice to do lying down as the feeling of your belly rising and falling is more pronounced. Gently close your eyes, or half close them if you prefer, and rest your awareness on your breath and lower belly area. Initially, you can place your palms on your belly area to connect with the movement of your belly as it rises and falls with each breath (or you can relax your arms in a comfortable position).

When you are ready, take a deep, intentional breath into your nose, filling up your body with air (without force) and feel your belly expand like a balloon. Follow this to the very top of the in-breath and then gently let your belly area relax and sink back downwards as you slowly exhale through the nose all the way out.

This will lead you to your next in-breath, which will expand your belly area again, followed by another sinking out-breath, where you feel your belly contract and relax again. Rest your full awareness on your lower belly area as you continue expanding and contracting with your breath. Nothing else matters now but your breath: your full focus is on your breath and belly. Feel a sense of new energy and vitality entering your body and mind with each in-breath and then feel a sense of release, or letting go, with each out-breath.

Continue this gentle inhaling (expanding) and exhaling (contracting) for 10 rounds or more—until you feel a deep sense of calm awareness—constantly working on making your breath slower, smoother and deeper with every round of breathing. Feel the gentle expansion and contraction of your belly as you pump freshly oxygenated blood through your body and brain. Rest in this space for as long as you feel the need to.

At the end of the practice, take your time to gently wriggle your fingers and toes as you start awakening new energy to your body. In your own time, gently open your eyes and take the calm awareness back into the rest of your day.

You can use this deep breathing technique when you're feeling a bit stressed, anxious or overwhelmed during the day. It is a great practice to ground you back into your body and help you re-centre. The more you do this practice, the more you train your ability to self-regulate and refocus. I recommend doing this practice a couple of times a day. It's a great one to go to bed with.

Note: Sometimes when you stop or slow down, your thoughts might get busier. If this happens, gently acknowledge them and bring your attention back to your breath and to your body as you expand and contract your belly area.

Practice 2: Box breathing

This is a similar technique, but you simply:

Make yourself comfortable.

Breathe in for a count of four.

Hold for a count of four.

Breathe out for a count of four.

Hold for a count of four.

Continue to repeat this for your chosen duration (e.g. two, five, 10 minutes).

CHAPTER 4

ON SELF-REGULATION

Self-regulation is the capability to remain calm in difficult situations, manage your emotions and adapt appropriately to your environment. As we saw in chapter 1, the first step to managing stress and preventing burnout is developing self-awareness. The second most effective step for preventing burnout is the ability to self-regulate. This chapter explores the concept of self-regulation and discusses what it is and why it's so important. I will also give you some practical tools on how to develop it.

Back roads of Uganda

The way to travel the back roads of Uganda and Rwanda is on the back of farmers' trucks as they travel through the country-side. You simply pay the driver a few dollars as you jump on and they drop you off en route to their destination. Sometimes you may share your ride with the farmers' beloved chickens and goats and other times with a group of noisy schoolchildren. It's mostly fun and you never know what's in store.

> **Self-regulation is the capability to remain calm in difficult situations, manage your emotions and adapt appropriately to your environment.**

On one particular late afternoon ride, the truck I was on was picking up young, male soldiers armed with rough-looking machetes and machine guns, some of which were held together with gaffer tape. I had a gut feeling that this was not going to be one of those fun rides. This seemed more like a case of being in the wrong place at the wrong time. Over the previous few days, I had noticed there were soldiers everywhere. It was during the time that the neighbouring Congolese president, Kabila, was allegedly killed by an 18-year-old child soldier and there was a lot of political unrest in the area. This was not a great time to be in this part of the world and I could feel the tension in the air as our truck was filling up with soldiers. To make matters worse, I could smell alcohol on their breath and they were becoming mischievous.

One of the young soldiers behind me decided to toy with me. He started nudging and provoking me from behind as he laughed with his comrades. I did not turn around. Suddenly, I felt a piercing stab in the back of my ribs. I froze in fear—*Is it a knife or a gun?* Without turning around, I glanced over my shoulder using my peripheral vision and saw it was his gaffer-taped machine gun poking hard into my rib cage. *Here we go again: fight or flight?* I asked myself. *Shall I jump off the truck and run?* Probably not—the soldiers would have toyed with me like wounded prey and besides, I was in the middle of nowhere! Fighting was out of the question: I had zero chance against these drunk soldiers and their makeshift weapons. I'd be killed. The adrenaline was surging through my body. I was shaking with fear and uncertainty.

I knew I needed to do something to self-regulate and get out of my panicked state. I decided to take three deep breaths before making any reactive decisions about what to do in this life-threatening situation. I took one big inhale, followed by a long, slow exhale, which calmed me down a little. I took a second deep inhale and an even slower releasing exhale, which seemed to last forever. It felt like the longest three breaths I'd ever taken. It wasn't until I let out my third exhale that it suddenly came to me what the best response might be in this situation. Humour! I recalled on previous corrupt border crossings and other tricky situations in Africa that a sense of humour goes a long way. So I came up with the crazy idea of playing 'Rock, paper, scissors' with the young soldier sitting in front of me.

I raised my hand and played a few rounds. This got a few smiles. The machine gun was still poking hard at my ribs, but I ignored it. I started playing with another soldier who reeked of sweat and cheap alcohol. I won three rounds in a row and got some laughter and bigger smiles. He demanded a rematch, which he won. Then, other soldiers started competing against each other and we continued the 'Rock, paper, scissors' competitions as we bounced along the potholed jungle road.

The mood was slowly softening, but the machine gun didn't budge. Next, I chose the scariest looking and biggest soldier near me and we played three rounds. He beat me hands down. This was met with louder laughter and even bigger smiles. And then something changed. I felt the gun subtly release from my ribcage and a tap on my shoulder. As I turned around, I was met with the gaze of the young soldier who had been tormenting me—he was motioning me to play the game with him. To my relief, he beat me four times and he was pleased. His big grin said it all. He even gave me a celebratory high-five.

Moments later, the truck reached a busy crossroads. All of the soldiers collectively jumped up and gave me more high-fives and smiles as they piled off the truck. I collapsed back against the truck tray in relief and looked up at a lone, elderly farmer holding a sack of plantain bananas who was smiling at me. *Phew, that was a close call!* I said to myself, relieved to be alive as my body started releasing the pent-up tension. This unnerving experience was a strong lesson for me in the power of the 'pause' and developing the capacity to self-regulate in any situation. It also further consolidated for me the need to never underestimate the power of the breath in terms of self-control!

Life lesson: Self-regulation

The ability to self-regulate gives you the choice to create the space to mindfully choose your response in any given situation rather than react. Pause, breathe, create space and respond mindfully, instead of reactively.

Types of self-regulation

As I touched on at the beginning of the chapter, self-regulation is the ability to monitor and manage your energy states, your emotions, your thoughts and your behaviours and then take the best decisive action in any given situation. Sometimes it requires you to take a pause between a feeling and an action: to think things through, assess the situation and make a plan of how to positively approach the situation to give you the best outcome.

There are three main types of self-regulation: sensory regulation, emotional regulation and cognitive regulation.

Sensory regulation

Sensory regulation is the brain's ability to calm down or become more alert depending on your needs in your immediate environment, or during the task at hand. It's also about being more aware of the sensations present in the body. This could be as simple as physically noticing when your shoulders are feeling tight or your back is sore from sitting at your desk for too long and consequently getting up for a stretch or a walk. It could also be when your senses are becoming overstimulated from too much work and you need to calm down and switch off for a moment.

Emotional regulation

Self-regulation may be referred to as emotional regulation when it relates to your capacity to manage your emotional responses and impulses. This is useful, especially with emotions like anger. Instead of having an angry outburst and reactively saying or doing something you might regret, if you are mindful you may be able to self-regulate and manage your response to express the anger in a more constructive way. Equally, if you are operating out of fear, you may demonstrate desperate or negative behaviours and make fear-based decisions rather than rational ones. When you are more aware and able to regulate these emotions you can remain calm even when under pressure.

Cognitive regulation

Cognitive regulation is the ability to control and sustain your thinking and attention, and to resist distraction. It's also about a set of behaviours, thoughts and beliefs towards the attainment of a goal. This could be your ability to stay focused for long periods of time without your attention waning or becoming distracted. You might spend sustained periods of time at work solving problems, thinking analytically, making decisions and using up all of your cognitive resources so that your mental focus and clarity are compromised.

In some of my corporate workshops I take groups through a simple body scan practice, which is a mindful practice of bringing awareness to different parts of the body and the sensations that might be present there. I am often amazed at the positive comments from participants after the short practice:

- I didn't realise how many aches and pains I had in my body.

- I wasn't aware of how much tension I was holding in my jaw and neck.

- I felt my shoulders drop five inches!

- I feel so calm and present.

- That overwhelming/anxious feeling has subsided.

- My headache has totally gone.

- I didn't realise how tired I was. I nearly fell asleep.

- I was feeling angry/upset when I came in but now that feeling has gone.

- I feel so much lighter and clearer in my mind.

All of this can be achieved by simply tuning in to your body and self-regulating through awareness of breath and body. This is where practising mindfulness enables you to become present with what is going on within and around you and in turn to do something about it by self-regulating.

Why is self-regulation so important?

In terms of stress management and preventing burnout, developing the capacity to self-regulate is very important. Everyday stressors are normal, and as long as you manage them on a daily basis, or even an hourly basis, they will not turn into chronic stress. Remember that burnout results from chronic stress not being managed; therefore, being able to manage your ability to self-regulate will prevent everyday stress from developing into chronic stress, potentially resulting in burnout.

Daily, or even hourly, stressors will keep coming at you every single day: emails, deadlines, priorities, workload and everything else that arises in the course of a workday. We have little control over the amount of incoming stress, but we do have full control over how we react to it when we develop our ability to self-regulate during the day. Stress can be positively motivating, and by frequently self-regulating throughout the day to manage your stress it will not accumulate over the week and leave you feeling depleted. Doing simple things like pausing every few hours when you're feeling overwhelmed, taking a renewal break when you're feeling fatigued, practising breath breaks or meditation when you're losing focus, changing your environment when you're feeling reactive, or going for a refreshing walk, will all help to self-regulate your energy and clarity.

> **We have little control over the amount of incoming stress, but we do have full control over how we react to it when we develop our ability to self-regulate during the day.**

As we have already established, the earlier on in the stress cycle you become aware of your stress, the easier it is to manage. If you catch it in the everyday stress stage (green zone), then using the self-regulating technique will be far more effective than waiting until the stress has reached the orange zone, where you are approaching fatigue and burnout. 'Nip it in the bud' as soon as you can with a simple technique before it evolves further and has damaging effects on your health and mental wellbeing.

A busy surgeon I work with is notorious for doing long operating shifts and often works 60- to 80-hour weeks. He used to ignore all the signs of stress resulting from his overwhelmingly busy days. He loves his work and especially loves being engaged in complex surgical procedures, so he did not feel the need to slow down. He divided his time between his private practice and a public practice, driving between various clinics and hospitals throughout the week. He was initially not aware of the consequences that this workload was having on his health because he loved it so much, and although he was mentally and physically exhausted at the end of the week, he said he still felt pretty good.

That was until he fell asleep at the wheel of his car for a few seconds after one of his long shifts. He woke up totally shocked. Fortunately, he only hit a garden hedge and no-one was hurt, apart from a few garden gnomes. This was the turning point for him, and he started taking renewal breaks every day, operated less frequently, slightly decreased his working hours and dramatically increased his self-care habits. He still works relatively long hours, but he is now more aware of what he needs to do to self-regulate on a daily and hourly basis.

He said that throughout the day he is constantly renewing his energy and feels more present and mindful of his daily workflow. He even does breathing practices while he is operating and does two-minute breath breaks while he is washing his hands between patients. By constantly renewing his energy throughout the day he doesn't feel exhausted at the end of the week. The other bonus he shared with me is that he doesn't fall sick every time he takes his annual leave holiday, which he normally would have in the past!

How to develop self-regulation

You can do many things to help calm yourself down and self-regulate, such as going for a walk, practising yoga, riding a bike, having a change of environment, getting a massage, doing artwork or anything that relaxes you.

The following is a small—though certainly not comprehensive—selection of mindfulness techniques to help you self-regulate during challenging times. These are simple but effective practices that I personally use and have shared with many people with positive results.

The 'Coming to your senses' exercise

One of the simplest ways to self-regulate, get yourself out of the reactivity of stress and come back to the present moment is through your senses. Say, for example, you are working away on your computer, starting to lose focus and feeling stressed and anxious about all the work ahead of you. Before you get swept away by your catastrophising future thoughts, and your anxiety, it's best to pause, take your hand off the mouse, place your hands on your lap, take your eyes off the computer and ask yourself the following five questions:

1. *What can I see right now?* Look around you and take in your environment.

2. *What can I hear right now?* Tune in to the soundscape around you, both near and far.

3. *What can I smell right now?* Notice the scents around your environment without judging them as good or bad.

4. *What can I taste right now?* Notice the tastes present in your mouth—perhaps you could have a drink, or pop a snack into your mouth and tune in to the taste and flavours.

5. *What do I feel right now?* Tune into the sensations of your body: feel your back against the chair, your hands on your lap and your feet on the ground.

This is a very grounding practice and only takes a few minutes. It helps you self-regulate by tuning back in to the present moment and can stop overwhelm in its tracks. It can instantly calm you down, slow down your heart rate and help relax your mind. It also helps you to become an observer of your mind rather than getting swept away by your thoughts. And the best thing is, you can do it anywhere, anytime.

Be comfortable with doing nothing

We all need some time out from constantly 'doing'. When was the last time you had five minutes to do absolutely nothing—and I mean *nothing*? So many people say to me that they wish they had more time, but the moment they get five minutes to themselves they fill it up with more activity. For example, you get a five-minute break at work so you start googling something on your computer, or you reach for your phone and start scrolling. Your mind is already full and busy, yet you fill it up with more stimulation and information, which only leads to more overwhelm and overload.

We take in more information in a single day than somebody in the 15th century would have taken in over a whole year. What's more, a PhD student's 2011 study published in *Science Express* found that we are exposed to the equivalent information of 174 newspapers per day![13] How can we possibly take it all in?

> **We take in more information in a single day than somebody in the 15th century would have taken in over a whole year.**

Think about a typical day. From the moment we wake up, we are busy checking our phones, reading or listening to the news on our commutes and scrolling the internet—not to mention all of the external bombardment of information that we are constantly over-stimulated by. Give yourself a little brain break and do absolutely nothing for a while so your mind can process some of this information. Take yourself outside, sit on a park bench (without your phone) and give yourself some space to 'just be' (not do) for a change. You might be amazed by how difficult it is to do nothing for five minutes—but you might be equally amazed at how much better you feel afterwards.

Create space with mindfulness

Somebody once asked me, 'What has been the biggest benefit for you regularly meditating for 30 years?'

I really had to stop and think about my response for a moment. I instantly thought of countless benefits, but it turned out that 'pausing and thinking about my response' was actually the answer. I replied, 'It helps me to create space between a stimulus and my response to that stimulus, and the more I meditate, the bigger that space becomes' (as we saw in the Uganda story at the beginning of this chapter). The more you train your ability to sit comfortably with yourself and be with your thoughts, the more you can feel comfortable to hold space in various situations. Have you ever noticed that your thoughts come and go, and have you noticed that there is a space between one thought and the next? The more you practise mindfulness and meditation, the more aware you become of that space and the more comfortable you are with it.

Our minds are so busy with thoughts and external stimuli that we have no capacity left for creative thoughts to arise. When you sit in a mindful meditation practice, you create space to *just be* for a while and observe the sensations and thoughts that arise without reacting to them. You can also take this practice 'off the mat' and into your everyday life to be more self-aware and less reactive to events that happen to you over the course of the day. When something happens to you in your day, it creates a stimulus that then triggers a reaction or a response. For example, one of your colleagues at work says something to upset you and you instantly snap back with your emotional response, or it might even be a terrible email that you respond to in anger. This is not a great way to operate and you are likely to regret what you said moments later. Often, the more stressed you are, the smaller the space between stimulus and response is. In an illustrative form, this looks something like figure 4.1 (note that there is no space).

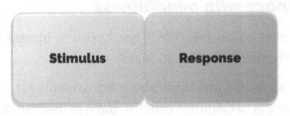

Figure 4.1 reactive response

Conversely, the more you train your awareness and ability to self-regulate with the mindfulness practices, the better you can 'create space' between this stimulus and response (see figure 4.2). For example, someone says something that upsets you and instead of snapping back angrily, you take a moment before you respond—it might only be the space of one breath or a polite pause. In this moment you create the space to allow a series of thoughts and processes to flow through your mind so that you can:

o   assess the present situation

o   look at the bigger picture

o   step back and create perspective

o   observe your mind without judgement

o   create a possible solution

o   have empathy

o   respond mindfully and respectfully.

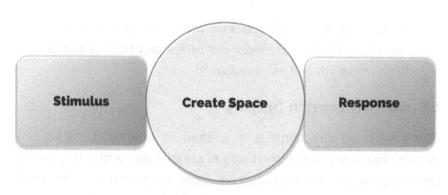

Figure 4.2 mindful response

A good example of this is Michael, a client and friend of mine and a Senior Director of a Melbourne-based financial institution, who has been working on self-regulation and the ability to create space for a while now. He says that he has gone from a three out of 10 to a six out of 10 and admits it is still a work in progress. One of the things that fires him up the most is traffic to and from work and he notices himself getting frustrated and angry when people cut him off. He is getting better at self-regulating, but sometimes he has to stay in his car at the end of his trip, and take five breaths to 'let go' of some of the built-up traffic frustration before he enters his workplace.

What I love about Michael is his honesty. He says he doesn't get it right all of the time, but he is continually working on it. I taught Michael some deep breathing techniques and he now doesn't get fired up anywhere near as often. It's a work in progress and long-term change takes patience and time but he is doing great.

One of my favourite books, which summarises this perfectly, is Viktor Frankl's *Man's Search for Meaning*. Frankl describes his time in the concentration camps during World War II. Even under the horrific conditions of being imprisoned in a concentration camp you still have a choice—you can choose your responses. He writes,

Between stimulus and response there is a space. In that space is our power to choose our response. In our response lies our growth and our freedom.[14]

90-second breath breaks

Along with all the benefits described in chapter 1, 90-second breath breaks are also a great way to create space and self-regulate instantaneously. Remember: give yourself permission to stop! Stopping for 90 seconds or so can make the world of difference to your overall energy and mood throughout the day. It's a great way to create space between stimulus and response, it can disrupt your reactive mode of working, and you can regain your focus and balance. The more frequently you have small breaks in your day, the more you train your capacity to disrupt the stress response and reset your intention to work more mindfully and purposefully.

Body scan practices

A very popular formal mindfulness practice is the body scan. This is one of the most effective practices for those starting out with mindfulness. The body scan is a great way to bring connection and awareness to your body and equally to your mind. This practice is beneficial when you're feeling disconnected, stressed or just want to relax.

The body scan practice is simply about bringing awareness to various parts of your body and noticing any sensations that might be present there. Often, by simply bringing awareness to a part of your body, you can release any tension that might be accumulating in that area. You do this portion by portion from your head down to your toes, or vice versa, bringing awareness to each region and gently letting go with your breath. You can do this practice seated or lying down.

The great thing about the body scan is that it only takes five to 10 minutes, yet it is very effective in releasing stress and reconnecting to your body and mind. It is a wonderful way to unwind after a busy day. Having said that, you can use this body scan at any time of the day: you can use it in the morning to bring vitality and presence to your day; at the end of your day to create space and unwind; or you can practise it before bedtime to get a good night's sleep. No matter which time of the day you choose to use the body scan practice, aim to do it at least once a day to reconnect with your mind and body and help you find balance.

You will find a body scan script at the end of this chapter.

The cumulative positive benefits

Making these small changes and doing these practices can have positive long-term effects on your mental health and wellbeing. The best feedback I ever received from somebody who initiated the body scan practice and other daily self-regulating techniques was from Jack, a hard-working business owner in the construction industry. He ran a large firm with more than 200 full-time employees as well as many sub-contractors. He felt overwhelmed managing multiple building sites and team members, which caused him some niggling anxiety most of the day. Jack had a spasmodic mix of physically demanding days on site and sedentary days in his office. He mentioned he was so 'out of tune' with his body that he often had chronic aches and pains, which impacted his sleep. He was so disconnected to the sensations and signals of his body that he sometimes totally forgot to eat during the day and he rarely stretched or exercised because he was constantly tired.

After only one month of doing the self-regulation techniques and a nightly body scan practice, Jack was amazed that his aches and pains virtually disappeared. He has made a concerted effort to eat well, which gives him the energy to exercise more frequently—and the best thing is, he sleeps an average of eight hours a night, especially when he does a body scan practice before going to bed. Jack still has stressful days and a lot to manage in his company but being able to self-regulate and manage the stress on a daily basis has made all the difference.

* * *

The wonderful thing about all of these effective and easily implementable self-regulation practices is that they take only minutes out of your day. All they require is your attention and a bit of practice. Developing an ability to self-regulate in various situations will have a profound effect on your everyday stress levels and mental wellbeing. Imagine working productively each day and achieving all of your demands without feeling wiped out at the end of the week so you still have the energy to enjoy your weekend. With mindfulness and self-regulation practices, all of this is possible.

Self-regulation practices

Choose one simple self-regulation technique from this chapter and aim to practise it regularly throughout your day. The more you practise, the better you will get at self-regulating during stressful, overwhelming or anxious times and the more you will avoid the onset of cumulative stress.

Practice 1, Technique 1: Coming to your senses

In moments of overwhelm, stress or anxiety, pause what you are doing and self-regulate by tuning in to your senses and becoming present to what you see, hear, smell, taste and feel right now. It's a great way to switch off your busy mind and reconnect to the present via your senses.

Practice 1, Technique 2: Creating space with mindfulness

Remember to create space between stimulus and response. It could be as simple as stopping in your car in the driveway before you enter your home after a big day of work, or it could be as subtle as taking a breath before responding to somebody in conversation. First of all, notice the triggers that might stimulate you into reactive behaviour and create space between the stimulus and your response.

Practice 1, Technique 3: 90-second breath breaks

I know we discussed this in previous chapters, but you can never do too many 90-second breath breaks. Continue to incorporate these into your day. Simply pause and follow your breath for 90 seconds to self-regulate throughout the day.

Practice 1, Technique 4: Be comfortable with doing nothing

Disconnect to reconnect! Give yourself some time to switch off devices and comfortably do nothing periodically during your day. Just take five minutes to unplug and give your mind a short brain break. Think of it as a little recharge moment. In the words of Anne Lamott, 'Almost everything works better when you unplug it, including you'.[15]

Practice 2: Body scan

Following is a script for the body scan, but you can also listen to the audio in the resources section at www.melocalarco.com/book. You might start with two or three times a week, and ideally build it up to daily if you are enjoying the benefits. This is a great practice to end your week or day with, or after you've finished a big project or a stressful day. Tune in to your body (and breath) to become present again and to reconnect to your body and mind.

Wherever you are, make yourself comfortable—whether that's standing, seated on a chair or lying down. Keep yourself in a relaxed and aware position.

Now gently close your eyes, or if you prefer them open, half-close them and empty your gaze. Take a moment to settle yourself into this position.

Start by generally noticing how your body is feeling, right here and right now.

Gently gather all your attention towards your body.

Try to reel in all thoughts that take you to the outside world and allow the outside world to gradually melt away and dissolve into empty space.

Notice your breath without necessarily changing it. Just let it rise and fall naturally, without force.

Begin by bringing your attention to the area around the top of your head and gradually we will work downwards through your body to the tips of your toes.

Focus on the area around the crown of your head. Feel a sense of lightness around your head and imagine that all the tension is gently dissolving away.

Then shift your awareness to your temples and forehead, imagining any tension, stress, headache or pain dissolving away, disappearing, as you bring attention to this part of the body. Imagine any tension in your head draining down through your body and into the ground.

Now bring your attention to the area around the ears and jaw. Maybe give your jaw a wiggle from side to side and gently let go of any tension or tightness in this area. Let the tension release and feel it leave your face.

Pause for a short while and feel your whole head, face and jaw feeling comfortable and relaxed.

Then shift your focus to the area around your neck and shoulders. This is an area where we usually hold a lot of stress and tension, but we are going to slowly let it all relax and release. Gently relax the shoulders. Perhaps lift them up gently and as they drop, imagine all the tension dissolving down into the ground or dissipating into the air.

As you do this, try to feel that any tension or weight that you are carrying in your shoulders melts away. Feel as though you are really letting go of all the tension that is being held in your shoulders.

Think to yourself, 'My neck and shoulders are now comfortable and relaxed'.

Now relax your arms and hands and imagine all the tension in these areas draining down to your fingertips and away from your body. (Feel a comfortable weight at any points of contact to the chair or ground.)

Now shift your awareness to your back, from the top of the spine right down to your tailbone. Focus on any area of tension that may have built up around this area. Then feel each vertebra relax, from your upper back, right down to your lower back, still feeling erect and strong, yet supple and relaxed.

Next, bring your attention to the front of your body, relaxing the face again—jaw and neck—and then focus on the area around the chest and stomach.

Try to identify if there are any areas of stress or tension in this part of your body. Imagine that all the tension softens and dissipates as you focus on it. The chest can hold onto a lot of emotions, such as anxiety, stress, grief and fear, so try to let go of any built-up tension in this area and feel a lightness instead.

Now shift your attention to the hips and legs, noticing how they feel. Are your sit-bones (that is, the points of contact to the seat or floor) even? Are your ankles and feet even? Allow any tightness to disperse downwards towards the ground. Relax your knees and ankles and feel the ground beneath your feet (or heels) and let all your tension dissolve into the ground.

Now, feel your entire body relax as you gradually scan down from the crown of your head all the way to the tips of your toes.

Feel your body as a whole. Connect the body, breath and mind and feel totally relaxed ... grounded ... peaceful ... and comfortable. Fully present and connected to your body as it sits in this comfortable position.

Savour this moment for a while and then, whenever you are ready, gradually bring your relaxation to a close by becoming aware of the aliveness of your body. You can start by making small movements, like wiggling your fingers and toes, and when you are ready, gently open your eyes and bring yourself back to the place where you are sitting or lying.

Appreciate this moment of calmness, relaxed awareness and presence of your body for the rest of the day or evening.

CHAPTER 5
ON OVERWHELM AND ANXIETY

Do you sometimes feel overwhelmed from juggling the many things in your life? Whether it's your demanding workload or your busy family commitments — or a combination of both — you are not alone. Many people today feel constantly overwhelmed and don't know what to do about it. Many people I speak to feel so overwhelmed that it creates a constant niggling underlying anxiety, which makes them feel out of control. Our fast-paced world has created more stress, more overwhelm and more feelings of anxiety than ever before and we need some tools and techniques to manage this. In this chapter we will explore this in a bit of detail and give you some applicable tools to help you find balance in our frantic world.

11 000 feet above South Australia

There I was, 11 000 feet in the air and strapped to my skydiving instructor for my first ever tandem skydive. It was something I had wanted to do for some time for the adrenaline rush and to embrace my fear (I sometimes have a fear of heights and I thought this could be a good way to face it). I must admit, I wasn't feeling great because I had had a big night out the evening before celebrating life and drinking far too many Jack Daniels. Not a great idea the night before a parachute jump!

As we ascended in the modest little Cessna plane, I felt a mix of fear, uncertainty, excitement and nausea, but I was ready for it. The door of the aircraft opened just like a car door and the blast of wind immediately woke up all of my senses. I was guided by the instructor to carefully step out of the plane and onto the wheel shaft to set myself up to jump. With nothing but a wheel shaft and thousands of feet underneath me, I was motioned to cross my arms over my chest and get ready to jump on the count of three. I must add that the guy who jumped before me hit his head on the wheel and was knocked out for part of his freefall, so that didn't help with my confidence.

1, 2...

On '3' I blacked out for a few seconds, overwhelmed and overstimulated by the sensory overload of everything going on around me. It was all too much for my body and mind to take in! I was thankful it was a tandem jump because I was totally out. I passed out for a few seconds and woke up in the middle of the freefall. The surge of adrenaline kickstarted me back into the present moment and it was exhilarating feeling the G-forces push my face into a permanent smile. I was loving it! Regaining my composure, I laughed and joyfully shouted with my instructor as we both free fell through the sky at the rapid pace of 200 feet per second—that's 190 kilometres per hour. 'Yoo-hoo, what an amazing feeling!'

Then, suddenly, he pulled the chute and everything slowed down as we were jolted into a feeling of pure bliss. The stimuli around me turned to peace and calm. It was like somebody had changed the TV channel as time stood still for a moment and my senses absorbed the peace and quiet around me. I felt my heart rate slow down and observed the landscape beneath me slowly come closer as I dropped peacefully through the sky. In this moment, all I felt was pure, joyful bliss! *Wow!* There I was, floating like a bird, taking in the awe-inspiring scenery beneath me as we slowly circled our way back to earth.

Everything leading up to this moment was superfluous and was quickly eliminated from my mind. All of the fear, worry, anxiety and overwhelm I had felt the night before and as we ascended in the small plane had been unnecessary. It was all created in my mind when, in actual fact, after the adrenalin rush of freefalling through space and time, everything else was pure enjoyment. The moment we hit the ground, like a kid on an amusement park ride, all I wanted to do was go straight back up and do it all again.

> **...everything that is meaningful and amazing in life is often on the other side of fear or discomfort.**

What did this teach me? That everything that is meaningful and amazing in life is often on the other side of fear or discomfort. And all of that fear, anxiety, worry and procrastination is only robbing you of these experiences. Yes, it was scary. Yes, it was overwhelming. Yes, it was challenging. But on the other side was joy, excitement, fulfilment, accomplishment and so much more.

Think of a time in your life when you spent the whole night worrying about something you had to face the next day—like a presentation you had to make, public speaking, a big meeting or a difficult conversation. You spend the whole previous night tossing and turning, perhaps worrying about all the things that could go wrong. You might be thinking things like, 'What if I stutter? What if I forget my words? What if I fail? What if I don't know the answers to their questions?' When in actual fact, the next day you complete the task and everything runs successfully and smoothly. With a sense of relief, you feel proud and happy with your achievements. Why did you need all that overwhelming worry the night before?

> ## Life lesson: Overwhelm and anxiety
>
> Overwhelm, worry and anxiety are often created in your mind. Instead of worrying about all of the 'what ifs' that may or may not happen, try to only focus on 'what is' happening in the present moment. You will always cope with that.

Overwhelm in the modern world

'Overwhelm' is probably one of the most common words that I hear in my line of work, and it is often one of the predecessors to anxiety and burnout. When I hear someone admitting they are overwhelmed, it's usually an orange flag: a sign they are not coping with their workload or they are trying to juggle too many things in their life. If someone vocalises their overwhelm, it usually means they are already struggling and are reaching out for help, so if you hear someone say they are overwhelmed, it may be worth offering them a helping hand. Or if you are feeling overwhelmed yourself, reach out for support. It's also beneficial to take a step back and break down what is causing the overwhelm in the first place. Then you can take some action towards managing it.

I regularly see this in the mental health clinics where I work. I often ask the inpatients as they engage in my programs how they are feeling and what led them to the clinic. Many respond by saying it was all too much, and they were feeling overwhelmed so they needed some support.

Our work lives have become increasingly challenging—tight deadlines, lack of resources, conflicting priorities, financial stressors, demanding workloads and the unrelenting pace of work life. We live in a world where we are always accessible and other people's demands for an immediate response are always hijacking our attention. Couple this with a busy home life juggling family needs, social events and all of the necessities of life and it can be completely overwhelming. Our typical response to these demands is to work even harder and put in longer hours, without breaks, to keep our head above water, often at the compromise of our own health.

Overwhelm can be defined as:

o being buried or drowned beneath a huge mass of something

o feeling defeated by something

o having too much to manage, too much to deal with

o experiencing loss of control

o feeling emotionally overloaded.

That's exactly what you might hear from people around you on a daily basis:

o I'm drowning in work.

o I can't see a way out.

o I just can't keep up with it all.

o It's all too much!

o It's manic at the moment!

o I never get to the end of my to-do list.

o I'm emotionally exhausted. I just can't do it all!

How creating a stress-reduction course stressed me out

I experienced this stress and overwhelm myself when I was working on a particular project that caused me some anxiety, which I had not experienced before. Ironically, it was while I was creating an online course titled 'Mindfulness for Stress Reduction.' Who would have thought that creating a course for stress reduction would actually cause me so much stress and overwhelm? Quite comical really!

I wanted to make the best possible course and I spent countless hours in the library after work researching and writing 12 modules. Each night I surrounded myself with medical journals, the latest research papers, mindfulness books and anything I could gather on the topic. I spent days, weeks and months doing this and I felt like I was getting nowhere. It was overwhelming me. I was buried under my papers and I was trying to do too much at once without any focus. It was truly stressing me out!

I eventually changed my approach and decided to be more mindful of what I was working on each evening by only working on one specific task with full focus. For example, if I was working on module 2b, then the only notes I would take with me were those on module 2b —nothing else. Before starting the work, I would do a Three-minute meditation practice to set my intention on what I was working on and to have a crystal-clear objective of what I wanted to achieve that night. This focused approach proved to be a good formula and I eventually finished the content for the course, which turned out to be Three months more of hard work and hundreds of pages of material.

I then went into creation mode with videographers, graphic designers and developers, and this proved to be an even more stressful experience. It cost me a lot of time, money and energy, but I will spare you the details here. Suffice to say I learned a great deal from this experience, and I could definitely feel the overwhelm turn to stress and then further manifest into feelings of anxiety. I must say, it took me a while to recover from this and I'm happy to say the course was successfully completed despite all of the challenges. You could imagine my apprehension about committing to writing this book with the word 'burnout' in the title. I jokingly tell people my next book will be titled *How I Nearly Burnt Out Writing a Book on Burnout!*

Our brains have a limited capacity. Cognitive overload is a state where we are given too many tasks or information at once and our brain cannot process all the information proficiently, which only leads to overwhelm and stress. We cannot perform our tasks with maximum efficiency and accuracy when we are operating in this distressed state. We keep taking on work—adding to our never-ending to-do list—and this leads to trying to multitask, which causes even more stress or anxiety. It's a perpetual problem and something we need to take control of. I'll share some tips on how to manage it later in this chapter.

The myth of multitasking

One of the biggest causes of stress is multitasking (or trying to). Research on multitasking over the past few decades states that:[16]

o multitaskers actually take longer to complete tasks and produce more errors

o multitaskers have difficulty retaining information

o multitaskers lose a significant amount of time switching back and forth between tasks, with productivity reduced by up to 40 per cent

o multitasking showed a drop of IQ of 10 points (which was similar to the effects of going without a full night's sleep, or going to work drunk)

o multitaskers have a deceived perception of being more efficient than they really are

o multitasking causes poorer academic results in students.

I run a corporate workshop on multitasking and at the beginning of the session I open with this innocent question: 'Who are the good multitaskers in the room?' Usually, the response is about 75 per cent raising their hands. After one hour of workshopping activities and having some fun along the way, I ask the exact same question at the end of the session and not one single hand is raised! Multitasking is a myth and not an efficient way to work!

Let's first differentiate some terms around multitasking to be clear on their meaning:

o *Unitasking:* doing one task at a time with 100 per cent of your attention focused on it (the best way to work)

o *Simple multitasking:* doing two simple tasks at the same time, such as driving the car and listening to music; or walking the dog and chewing gum; or simply walking and talking. Easy, right? We can handle that, can't we?

o *Complex multitasking:* trying to do two complex tasks simultaneously that require your cognition—for example, taking directions on a telephone conversation while somebody else is talking to you and giving you different complex instructions that you need to retain. We cannot do that! The human brain cannot do two cognitive tasks at the same time. This is where the problem lies because we sometimes think we can and we try to do multiple tasks simultaneously, which only leads to frustration, stress and overwhelm.

o *Context switching:* this feels like you are multitasking, but you are actually just switching your attention from one task to another. You can train yourself to get more efficient at this, but there is usually a price to pay when you are continually context switching throughout the day—and that price is inefficiency and feeling wiped out at the end of the day!

○ *Attentional blink:* when you are context switching from one task to another and in between tasks the brain goes offline for up to 0.05 of a second, during which time it does not take in information[17]. For example, you open the fridge to get an ingredient and you stand there for a moment scratching your head, or you are going from a call to your inbox and you take a moment to get back on track again. These attentional blinks get longer the more stressed you are. We want to minimise the amount of context switching and attentional blinks we have in a day.

Some interesting research around the cost of context switching states that if you quickly check your email while working away on another task—for example, you get a pop-up notification on your screen—it takes an average of 64 seconds to get your attention back on track again to what you were previously doing[18]. This might not sound like very long, but if you get interrupted every five minutes in a 40-hour working week—which I think is conservative because we often get interrupted much more often than that—guess how much time you lose in a week due to context switching? A whopping 8.5 hours—that's a whole day!

Not only that, but we feel unproductive, unfocused, stressed and overwhelmed and we get to the end of the day and say, 'What did I actually achieve today?' Just like my example of working in the library on my online course, you will also feel totally exhausted at the end of the day from reactively switching your attention from task to task all day long and not getting anything completed. You might spend so much of your day 'putting out fires' and constantly meeting other people's demands that you don't have time to do any of your own work, which creates further stress and anxiety. This is not a productive way to work and if you continue to operate in this way you may eventually burn out from the constant wear and tear on your body and mind.

I was discussing this with a friend, John Rowland, who is Senior Vice President of CGI, UK North and Australia, which is one of the largest IT and business consulting companies in the world with over 84 000 employees globally. I asked John how he stays focused and energised even though he is working across multiple time zones and managing a multitude of tasks every day (due to the time difference he sometimes has to work up to 18 hour days). Refreshingly, he said that the first thing he keeps a check on is his self-care, making sure he is exercising regularly, eating well and sleeping well no matter what life throws at him in his busy weeks. He understands that if he has long, demanding days at work, he has to balance those out with periods of renewal wherever possible—for example, taking a half day off and going for a 10-kilometre walk, or just taking time out on his farm. He says, 'You cannot be performing at your best if you are not at your best health wise.'

... sometimes you just have to take a step back and view things with a broader and wider lens to gain perspective.

He went on to say that you must also be clear on what you are working on and when. He doesn't believe in never-ending to-do lists: they just add to your stress because you continually add to them. He does not multitask; instead, he creates distinct objectives that he'd like to achieve in a clear, prioritised order and then he stops for 10 minutes and closes his eyes. For five minutes he does a quiet meditation and for the other five minutes he visualises an upcoming task. Sometimes, he says, when he opens his eyes, he alters his objectives or eliminates something from his tasks. Stopping for those 10 minutes gives him the clarity and focus to work on his tasks with laser-sharp attention for the next few hours. I loved an analogy John used about the problem of getting caught up in the busy-ness of reactively working all day long without any clear focus. He said, 'Sometimes you have to get off the dance floor and climb up onto the balcony to look down to gather some perspective.' I couldn't agree more: sometimes you just have to take a step back and view things with a broader and wider lens to gain perspective.

Anxiety

Anxiety is very complex and comes in many forms: social anxiety, general anxiety disorder, separation anxiety, panic attacks and other forms. There are many contributing factors that can create anxiety, but for the sake of containing this discussion we will mainly focus on generalised anxiety disorder (GAD), which is one of the most common forms, especially in the workplace.

Anxiety is something that many of us feel from time to time. It's our body's way of preparing us for a challenging situation—a bit like the fight-or-flight response. It is totally normal to feel anxious or nervous for a short period of time until it passes naturally—for example, before a job interview or public speaking. It's perfectly normal if anxiety comes and goes; the problems arise when the anxious feelings persist for a prolonged period of time.

GAD is characterised by experiencing some of the following symptoms and behaviours for a prolonged period of time (usually about six months):

- a constant state of worry about a variety of everyday situations
- irritability and restlessness
- muscle tension or body aches
- difficulty concentrating and paying attention
- sleep disturbances
- easily fatigued

- o withdrawal from friends and social events

- o feeling of unease (physically and mentally).

Furthermore, some people may experience panic attacks, where a sudden rush of intense anxiety or fear overcomes them. They might feel sensations like a pounding heart, tight chest, difficulty breathing, dizziness, sweating, nausea, shaking and so on. They might say things like, 'I can't breathe!' or 'I think I'm going to die!' Panic attacks can happen at any time and are usually the end result of unresolved stress accumulating in the body.

Somebody who had a very public panic attack was Dan Harris. It wasn't just any panic attack though. It was in front of millions of viewers worldwide while he was delivering the news as an anchorman on *Good Morning America* in 2004. In his book *10% Happier*[19], Dan describes how his panic attack on national television changed his life because it led him on a journey to find meditation to tame his mind and reduce stress. He was an absolute sceptic about meditation initially and that's what I love about the book. He views meditation through a humorous, sceptical lens and shares how it changed his view and calmed his anxiety.

'What if' thoughts

Feelings of overwhelm and anxiety can come from overthinking or catastrophising about the future, especially when things are out of your control. I often ask my clients what's causing their worry or anxiety and most of the time it is about a future event that may never even happen. However, it's easy to get so caught up in your thoughts, and create such a story around them, that it feels real and you believe it unequivocally. Some even joke to me that they are the 'masters of worry' and create catastrophising thoughts in their head. They can follow the thread so deeply into the realms of darkness that it feels like it is reality. Many times they are creating 'what if' thoughts, and they get carried away by them and follow them five layers deep. For example:

Layer 1: What if my performance review doesn't go well?

Layer 2: What if I lose my job?

Layer 3: What if I can't provide for my family?

Layer 4: What if I can't pay my mortgage (or rent)?

Layer 5: What if my whole family doesn't have anywhere to live?

And so on, and so on...

Who can relate to this? Are you good at creating lots of 'what if' scenarios in your mind?

There is no solution to worrying about the future *because it isn't real*—how can you possibly have to cope with something that hasn't even happened yet? Yes, you make contingency plans for when something goes wrong, but there is no benefit at all from worrying about all the things that can go wrong. Eckhart Tolle puts it so well in his bestselling book *The Power of Now*, in which he describes the future as a 'mental phantom':

> *Are you worried? Do you have many 'what if' thoughts? You are identified with your mind, which is projecting you into an imaginary future situation and creating fear. There is no way that you can cope with such a situation because it doesn't exist. It's a mental phantom...*

> *... Ask yourself what 'problem' you have right now, not next year, tomorrow, or five minutes from now. What is wrong with this moment? You could always cope with the Now, but you can never cope with the future—nor do you have to. The answer, strength, the right action or the resource will be there when you need it, not before, not after.[20]*

Powerful words that resonate with me for two reasons. One because they are so true, and two because they remind me of a client and good friend of mine, Chris, whom I was helping deal with a cancer diagnosis some years ago. He pointed out this particular page to me and said he read it over and over again to remind himself to just deal with the 'now', moment by moment, and not to worry about the future days, weeks or years ahead of him. Chris and I worked together every single day for his 49 days of assertive, targeted radiotherapy and chemotherapy to treat his aggressive throat cancer. Together we met each new day as it unfolded to do a variety of practices and techniques ranging from meditation, breathwork, Qigong, prayer, stretches and affirmations to sometimes just talking. Some days were tougher than others, but Chris has the strongest will and discipline of anyone I've met and he greeted each day with full presence and a positive mindset.

Other people, including some doctors, had told Chris the worst-case scenarios, saying things like, 'By week 2 you won't be able to eat solid foods; by week 3 you'll be having smoothies and your throat will be red-raw; by week 5 you'll have scars and burns everywhere; by week 6 you'll be wiped out and by week 7 you'll feel so bad that you wished you were dead!' We did not succumb to such negative words. We continued meeting each new day with positive intentions. Chris ate solid foods throughout his treatment, he managed to work most days and he kept up his normal routine as much as he could.

A few weeks after the last treatment, Chris kept up his oncology visits and medical check-ups while also continuing to run his successful businesses. He just kept powering on. His oncologist told Chris that in his 40-odd years of oncology, he had never seen anybody come out as unscathed and as positive as him. The oncologist said, 'I'm not sure exactly what you did to manage it so well, but it obviously worked!' It did not take Chris long to make a full recovery and he still lives life to the fullest — stronger, fitter and mightier than ever! A testament to meeting the challenges of each new day as it arose and not creating worry or anxiety about the future.

What's the benefit of worrying about all the things that might go wrong, or spending your mental energy consumed by 'what if' thoughts? It's better to focus your attention on 'what is' happening and what you have some control or influence over. Dealing with any situation day by day and moment by moment is a much healthier approach than catapulting your thoughts into a worrying future. If you spend your mental energy focusing on all the things you can't control, it will only create fear, worry and anxiety. This is where mindfulness practice is also beneficial because it helps you to stay present with 'what is' happening and deal with it appropriately when the need arises.

I learned this lesson very well on my cycling and travelling adventure around the world. I could not have foreseen all of the challenges that I was to face over the course of the next two years. Instead, I trusted that I would always have the right resources inside of me in the moment to deal with any situation, no matter how difficult, when the need arose. This has proven to be the best approach to life in general and I continue to adopt this outlook.

Ask yourself these questions:

o   Do I worry about a future that hasn't happened yet and create anxiety?

o   What do I do when I feel overwhelmed: does it consume me or can I manage it?

Another question to ponder:

o   Is it possible to be fully present and anxious at the same time?

Managing overwhelm

If burnout is the outcome of unmanaged workplace stress, and overwhelm is the consequence of not managing your daily workload and mental energy, then we need to put some strategies in place to manage this initial overwhelm before it progresses.

We could use the analogy of a tangled-up ball of wool full of knotted-up stress, overwhelm and confusion that then progresses to anxiety.

It looks something like the illustration in figure 5.1.

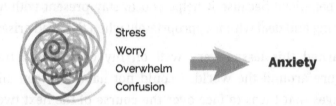

Figure 5.1 the evolution from overwhelming thoughts to anxiety

We want to catch overwhelm in the messy confusion stage and unravel it to see what is causing all the stress. In this way we can take decisive action before the overwhelm turns into anxiety. It's like untangling a big, messy knot of overwhelming thoughts and as you untangle it, you deal with each little individual knot one by one to see what's behind these thought knots. Is it worrying about the future? Is it trying to do too many things at once (multitasking)? Is it lack of focus? Is it too many external distractions? Is it being over-reactive? Is it pressure? Once we can untangle the knots and discover what the root cause of the stress is, we can find solutions.

Here are some valuable tips to get you started:

○ *If it's too many distractions while working,* manage the environmental distractions around you as much as possible.

For example, create a clutter-free workspace, put your phone away or on silent, mute your pop-up email notifications, communicate with your team that you are busy finishing a project, be crystal clear on what single task you are working on and stay on track as much as possible. Set yourself a focus time and stick to it.

○ *If it's an overwhelming to-do list,* take five minutes to review your list. Pick out the high-priority items, group other things into sub-groups—for example, phone calls, emails, quick-win tasks. Be realistic about what you can achieve in a day and allocate blocks of time to complete these tasks. Set clear intentions on what you are working on, catch yourself trying to multitask and pull yourself back to the task at hand. Also, acknowledge the completion of tasks and take renewal breaks often. Most people only look at what is still on their to-do list and don't savour the things they have achieved over the course of their day.

○ *If it's worrying about the future and all the things you still have ahead of you,* try not to project yourself too far into a future that you have little control over. Bring yourself back to the task at hand and only work on that. If it's a big project that takes days or weeks, break the project down into small, manageable tasks. The moment you catch yourself worrying about all the things ahead of you, take a few breaths and reset your focus back on the task at hand. Enjoy the creative process of working mindfully through each task.

○ *If it's feeling tired and not being able to keep going,* take a break, whether it's a tea/coffee break or a quick walk, a short meditation or just a chat with a colleague or friend. Give yourself permission to stop for a moment, change environment and renew your energy before you sit down again. Perhaps you can reprioritise what you are working on to make it more manageable. Feeling tired is usually a sign that you are not taking care of yourself. Check in with your diet, sleep and exercise routines.

o   *If it's competing priorities or looming deadlines,* manage this as best you can by allocating time based on the highest priority. Minimise distractions, have a clear timeline for each deadline marked out in your diary for the upcoming week/s, seek support wherever possible and manage your mental and physical energy. Do the hardest cognitive task earlier in the day when you are mentally at your freshest.

o   *If it's just keeping up with everything at work and home,* create clear boundaries as much as possible between work and home. Have a regular switch-off time when you no longer check emails and devices at home and reduce the temptation of working late at night just to keep up. Make sure you give yourself some downtime so you can function better the next day at work. Your home should be your place of rest and restoration. Reclaim that as best you can: do homey things like cooking, being with your family, reading a book and relaxing.

Managing anxiety

Getting back to that knotted mess of thoughts we were just talking about, the first thing I will say is to be more aware of your thoughts. Catch the stressful, overwhelming and confusing thoughts before they progress into physical feelings of anxiety. Research published in *Nature Communications* (2020) reveals we have about 6000 thoughts per day[21], and many of those

... you are not your thoughts.

thoughts are repetitive—that is, the same ones you had yesterday and the day before. Also, about 80 per cent of our thoughts are negative ones—this is based on our negative bias, which makes us look for danger or threats.

So, first of all, it's important to be more mindful of your thoughts. What is going on up there in my mind? What thoughts are swirling around in my brain hour by hour? What thoughts take me away from the present moment? What thoughts invoke certain feelings in me? What thoughts stress me out? What thoughts make me anxious? Turn towards your thoughts and observe them.

The second thing is to realise that *you are not your thoughts.*

Thoughts are just thoughts—that's all they are. It's up to you whether you give energy to negative thoughts and which ones you choose to let go of. I know it's easier said than done and will take some practice, but once you become more mindful of your thoughts and you can observe what thoughts come and go in your mind, you are better able to manage them. With mindfulness you can become an 'observer' of your mind and your thoughts rather than be swept away by them. You are also better equipped to turn towards your thoughts and question them, whether they are useful or not. Mindfulness gives you that choice not to judge a thought as 'good' or 'bad' but just to observe it.

I have a very straightforward formula that will catch almost 100 per cent of your overwhelming, negative, fearful or anxious thoughts. It is almost too simple yet it's hard to believe how effective it is. I share this with many of my clients, especially those suffering from anxiety, and I also often practise this formula myself. The formula works like this: if I am having a negative, fearful or anxious thought that is creating some tension or stress in my body, the first thing I do is turn towards that thought and ask it two very simple questions (see figure 5.2, overleaf).

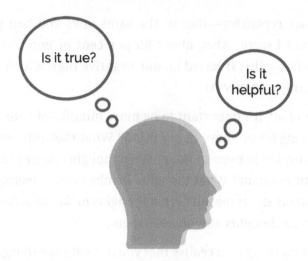

Figure 5.2 the formula for dealing with overwhelming, negative, fearful or anxious thoughts

Source: Head image: © Pogorelova Olga/Shutterstock

Question 1: Is it true?

Is it real? Is it a fact? What hard factual evidence is there to support it? For example, if I'm having a 'what if' thought about my presentation the following day, such as 'What if the group doesn't like my presentation and it falls flat?', I ask myself:

Is it true? Is it real? Is it a fact? No!

However, sometimes you may be able to justify that anxious, negative and fearful thought and say, 'yes, maybe it's true.' So then you ask the second question.

Question 2: Is it helpful?

Is it even useful or helpful for me to think this thought? Is it helpful for me to feed this thought? In the presentation example above, what's the point of thinking they won't like the presentation? It's not useful or helpful and will not put me in the right mindset.

This simple, straightforward formula helps me immensely and has helped thousands of people I have worked with over the years. It really is a gamechanger and makes all the difference as to how you manage your thoughts and the feelings associated with them. Observing any thoughts that are not serving you well will disempower them, and they will not further manifest into something bigger. Remember, you are not your thoughts. They are simply thoughts and it is up to you to be more mindful of them and choose your response.

I was chatting with Nick Bracks about this. Nick is an actor (*Neighbours*), mental health advocate and author of *Move Your Mind*[22]. He is also no stranger to experiencing anxiety himself and is a self-confessed 'overthinker.' As a child, Nick had several bouts of depression and anxiety and he speaks openly about this because he wants to help others who suffer mental health issues. Nick was often in the media spotlight as the son of a former Victorian premier, Steve Bracks. He noticed he often put a lot of pressure on himself, was a people pleaser and had a very busy mind. Nick explained to me that once he was able to 'turn towards' his thoughts and better understand the triggers that were causing his anxiety, he was also better able to deal with it. He said that the things that helped him deal with anxious moments best were creating regular exercise routines, practising meditation, observing his thoughts, calling a friend and practising gratitude and positive affirmations. I shared some breathing practices with Nick to help him calm his overactive mind and manage his overwhelm and anxiety.

If you are feeling moments of overwhelm or anxiety, or if you just have an overactive mind, pause and turn towards it. Take a moment to observe your thoughts and ask yourself those simple questions: 'Is it true?' and 'Is it helpful?' And don't forget to use the breathing techniques I taught you in the previous chapters to help calm your busy mind.

Overwhelm- and anxiety-busting practices

To manage feelings of overwhelm and anxiety before they manifest into something worse, you can combine the following four exercises. The more you can unravel the stressor and turn towards it, the better you can understand what is causing it and the more efficiently you can manage it.

1. Ditch multitasking

Trying to do too many things at once will only exacerbate your stress and overwhelm. Catch yourself, catch yourself, catch yourself, time and time again, when you find yourself trying to multitask, and pull yourself back to the one task you are working on.

2. Focus on 'what is', not 'what if' thoughts

Again, catch yourself when you are feeling swept away by future 'what if' thoughts that might be causing uncertainty and anxiety. Come back to the present moment and ask yourself *what is* really happening in this moment and how you can best deal with it. And remember, you can always deal with 'what is' happening, no matter how difficult it is.

3. Turn towards your thoughts

Remember that thoughts are just thoughts—that's all they are—and you have the choice to entertain those thoughts or to let them go if they are unhelpful. Always start by asking each anxious thought:

Is it true?

Is it helpful?

This will catch most of your negative, overwhelming and anxious thoughts and help you gain a deeper understanding of your thought processes.

4. Practise breathing

Don't forget the breathing practices you learned in the previous chapters as these will help you control your physiology during anxious moments and manage stress better.

CHAPTER 6

ON FEAR AND TRUST

Operating out of fear is very taxing on our energy systems and can be a contributing factor to burnout. Fear can make us procrastinate, preventing us from creating changes in our life, and it can hold us back from realising our full potential. Just like thoughts, when we turn towards our fear, we can better understand what is creating the fear and we can develop a better relationship with it.

In this chapter, I'd like to share a story about turning towards fear and also give you some techniques to embrace fear as a positive emotion to move forward in life. We will also explore the concept of trust as a way to flip your fears.

Kathmandu, Nepal

Something was wrong. Our usually friendly, smiling guesthouse host, Dillu, didn't even look up to greet us as we headed out to the streets of Kathmandu's tourist hub, Thamel, to buy our morning chai and breakfast. This was our first morning back in Thamel since completing a tiring but amazing 15-day trek in the Himalayas and all we wanted was a hearty breakfast and a warm chai tea.

As we walked out onto the street, Kila, my travelling companion, turned to me and said, 'Something is not right; it's too quiet.' Usually, the first sound we heard as we walked out of the Yeti guesthouse was the hypnotic Buddhist prayer, *Om Mane Padme Hum*, from the corner CD shop, which played it on repeat, but on this day there was no music. The mood on the street was sombre. The usually bustling shops and street vendors had their garage doors closed and there were very few people around. There was no music playing in the alleyways, no incense burning, no noisy street hagglers touting their wares, no food or chai scents wafting through the air. There was no-one anywhere on the streets, which usually buzzed with excitement and noise.

We noticed one of the local street vendors, whom we had got to know over the weeks, packing up her small shop. 'Excuse me, what is going on?' we asked her, as tears ran down her wrinkled face. Without looking up she muttered in broken English, 'The king is dead!' We helped her pack the rest of her goods into her trolley and sadly waved her goodbye.

Shocked from this news, we headed to the famous Pilgrims Bookstore, where many fellow travellers, backpackers and trekkers congregated to share stories, read mountain trekking books and sip warm chai together. In total disbelief, we discovered the horrible news that not only was the king dead, but also the whole Nepalese royal family had been brutally massacred. It was horrifying!

From the limited media coverage that we could access, we gathered the information that the previous night (1 June 2001), Prince Dipendra allegedly put on his military clothes and walked through the Royal Palace with a machine gun, gunning down his father, King Birendra, his mother, Queen Aishwarya, and several other members of the royal family, including his little brother and sister, before turning the gun on himself. The whole Nepalese monarchy was literally wiped out overnight, with 10 dead and five wounded in the massacre.

The most bizarre part was that while the perpetrator, Prince Dipendra, lay on life support in hospital he was crowned king of Nepal because he was the next heir to the throne. He reigned as king for three days before dying on 4 June. This unusual event turned the usually peaceful Himalayan kingdom upside down as the Nepalese people really loved their revered King Birendra. In the days that followed, things got progressively worse as grief-stricken people took to the streets of Kathmandu, rioting and expressing their confusion and anger towards the Nepalese government as the police started imposing military curfews. The normally peaceful country was now in a state of shock and hysteria.

As ever-threatening curfews were starting to be put in place, we decided to take one last trip to the nearby Monkey Palace for a bit of respite from the shocking news. Little did we know that the route to the Monkey Palace was also where the funeral procession for the king was being held. We came across a crowd of thousands of people paying respects to the king and the royal family, so we decided to join in. It was a fairly peaceful procession with many local people coming out from their rural villages to pay respect to their beloved king.

Then, only minutes later, the whole scene turned terribly ugly. We heard loud shouting, screaming children and ear-piercing gunshots: 'boom, boom, boom!' We weren't sure what was happening because we couldn't understand what the people were screaming as they fled in all directions, dodging the bullets and large rocks that were being hurled around us.

I instantly felt adrenalin surge through my body, sending blood pumping to all of my limbs, but I didn't know which way to run. I looked at Kila and saw a look of absolute fear and terror on her face like I had never seen on anyone before. I knew this was serious as I squeezed her hand tightly and we ran away in panic following the other fleeing people. Suddenly a hurling rock the size of my fist flew past my face, missing me by centimetres as I froze in shock. Then, more gunshots booming around us sent us back into a fleeing panic. We did not know where to run. I was just about to kick in the door of a small village house to seek refuge when an old woman, also hiding in fear, peeped out of the window, so we moved on.

The scene got worse as some of the men started fighting with each other. We saw angry men violently shaking a car and tipping it over on its end. We were amid a full riot and the scene was made worse by the sight of young, shaven-headed males raising their fists in the air in anger. We later learned that young males in Nepal shave their heads to show their respect and honour for the king.

Squeezing Kila's hand even tighter, I really didn't know what to do. We were so confused, so fearful, so uncertain in this fully blown riot. Which way to run: left, right, up, down or hide somewhere? Then, out of nowhere, a middle-aged man, whom we recognised as one of the street vendors in Thamel, also recognised us and motioned with his hands for us to follow him. I sensed that he had seen this type of riot before, having grown up among various political unrests and Maoist uprisings. We could see that he genuinely wanted to help us. We put our absolute trust in this kind man with his hardened but gentle face as he kept us close by his side. The frightening thing was that he motioned us to follow him towards the oncoming crowd instead of away from it. My natural instinct was to go the other way, but we followed him towards the angry rioting mob and just as we were metres away from it, we slowly snuck down the side of the street, which led us to a polluted river bank. We put 100 per cent trust in this man as we followed him, wading knee deep through a smelly sewage-polluted river. I would hate to think what was floating through that river as our feet sloshed through the black, oil-slicked mud and sewage, but we didn't care because we could hear the enraged sounds and fearful cries of the crowd behind us as we left the war zone.

Eventually we were led back through the dark back alleyways of Thamel and towards the familiar streets around Durbar Square near our Yeti guesthouse. The generous man then left us, placing his hands in front of his heart in prayer position and saying, 'Namaste'. We reciprocated the gesture, expressing our gratitude for the kindness of this stranger, who had saved our lives. Shocked and relieved, we stopped in at Kathmandu Guesthouse, which was one of the few places still open, washed our disgustingly toxic feet, and gathered our senses with a shot of whiskey while chatting with other puzzled and distraught fellow travellers. Sure that we had just escaped death, we felt a sense of relief come over us, as we tried to obtain information via the local news, the BBC and other sources.

The following days things went from bad to worse. All of the shops, eateries and guesthouses remained closed. There was no food or clean drinking water to be found, so many of us foreign travellers were getting progressively sick as we tried to survive and make an exit plan from Nepal. There were violent clashes on the streets, regular tear gas explosions, burning car tyres and roadblocks, and the streets of Kathmandu resembled a war zone. We heard the government had instilled a curfew with 'shoot at sight' orders and nobody was to be out on the streets for any reason whatsoever.

After many failed attempts, we finally made our way to Kathmandu airport and after literally kicking and fighting our way through built-up airport crowds, we eventually managed to get a flight out to Delhi. As our plane took off over the deserted streets of Kathmandu, I gazed out of the small window and the only movement I could see below was a few military trucks and soldiers as they patrolled the streets. As the flight levelled out, I turned to Kila and said, 'Phew, let's find some peace and quiet in Delhi'. 'Delhi' and 'quiet' are two words that I wouldn't usually use together in a sentence, but compared to what we had just experienced it seemed appropriate!

> **On the other side of fear there is trust.**

This experience in Kathmandu taught me some very valuable lessons that served me well for the rest of my travels—and for my life, for that matter. Throughout my travels I came across many more events that involved guns, knives and near muggings and the best option was always to turn towards the situation and meet it head on instead of running away from it. The other lesson was to always trust myself—trust that I will have what it takes to confront challenges—and also to trust my instincts when it comes to the kindness of others.

Life lesson: Fear and trust

On the other side of fear there is trust. Turn towards your fear and trust that you will always have the resources you need to get through any situation, no matter how difficult.

Primal fear

Fear is one of the most primal of human emotions and is usually triggered when we are in danger, under attack or in anticipation of a threat. Fear is programmed into our nervous system and puts our senses on high alert. It can trigger the stress response to flood our body with stress chemicals such as adrenalin and cortisol. This is a handy mechanism to engage when we are under attack and need to survive a threatening situation, but it is not a good way to operate all day, every day.

Just like stress, fear can be both motivating and debilitating. In some ways, I love travelling in developing countries because this is where I feel most 'alive'. That's not to say I put myself into dangerous situations, but when they arise, my senses are on high alert and I feel most alive. It's probably the same mechanism that motivates people to perform extreme sports, such as base jumping, caving, freediving, wingsuit flying, cliff diving and all of those adrenalin-fuelled sports that put your life on edge. There is an addictive high associated with this, but fear can also sap you of all of your energy, leaving you feeling depleted. Continually operating out of fear for prolonged periods of time can tax your energy so much that it could lead to burnout.

Some of our biggest fears are:

o   fear of inadequacy

o   fear of rejection

o   fear of uncertainty

o   fear of change

o   fear of missing out (FOMO)

o   fear of being judged

o   fear of losing control

o   fear of being hurt—for example, love or loss

o   fear of failure.

This might explain why the number-one fear for humans is public speaking. It ranks higher than the fear of dying: if you look at the above list, public speaking involves most of our biggest fears.

Which of these fears have you been able to relate to at certain times of your life?

Demystifying fear and understanding it better

Fear is often debilitating and people who spend their life in fear have immense trouble moving forward. They may procrastinate over big decisions, feel stuck, feel trapped and cannot progress in life.

Operating out of fear is not a healthy way to approach work or life. I'm not only talking about life-threatening fear like that described in the story above, but also fears that arise in the workplace or at home. Sometimes you might spend your days operating out of so much fear and uncertainty that you feel anxious at the slightest thing: the telephone rings and you think the worst, anticipating bad news; or your email pings and before you even open it you feel your heart pounding. You feel jumpy and on high alert all day long.

We can have fear of failure, fear of making mistakes, fear of not meeting our expectations, fear of losing our job, fear of losing somebody, fear of getting sick, fear of having a difficult conversation, fear of many things. Everybody experiences fear differently and the trouble is we can have a myriad feelings, emotions and behaviours associated with fear, which can cause some confusion. Figure 6.1 shows a few examples of feelings and behaviours associated with fear.

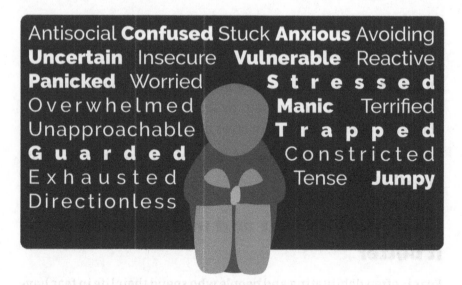

Figure 6.1 fear can affect us all differently

I'm sure you can add some words of your own to this list.

Ask yourself what your relationship with fear is and how you feel and behave when you are scared.

It's hard to change your emotional response if you are not sure what exactly you are feeling. However, if you can drill your fear down to the primary emotion, you can then better understand it and take some action towards it. For example, you might feel 'stuck' in your life for various reasons, creating different emotions. Perhaps you are stuck in sadness, unmotivated and depressed; or you are stuck in the past, which is holding you back; or you could be stuck in fear of taking the next step into the unknown. These are very different reasons for feeling stuck, so it is beneficial to open your awareness to what the primary emotion is that you are feeling so you can work directly with that emotion.

Ask yourself the question, 'What do I do when I'm confronted with fear?'

Do you push it away, do you run away from it, do you procrastinate, do you freeze or do you embrace it?

Further ask yourself, 'What am I really afraid of and what is the worst-case scenario that could result from this situation? Is it a matter of life and death? Is the fear real or perceived?' Quite often, the fear is perceived and the more we feed the fear with more uncertainty and anxiety, the more the fear continues to grow rapidly. Developing an open-minded relationship with fear is a great asset.

Embracing fear in the workplace

As a high performer in the workplace there is also an addictive nature to pushing yourself out of your comfort zone, making courageous decisions, motivating a team and constantly dealing with fear and uncertainty. This is especially true when things go right: it is rewarding, challenging and fulfilling, but it is also resource heavy and it takes away a lot of your energy, so you need to be aware of your limits. When working in a high-pressure job or faced with a challenging situation it's important to embrace the unknown and push your limits, but it's equally important to manage your personal energy along the way.

> **... you need to embrace the uncomfortable and turn towards the fear of managing uncertainty.**

I was discussing this with Scott Chapman, CEO of the Royal Flying Doctor Service, Victoria, who is no stranger to embracing fear and uncertainty in his personal and professional life. Scott has spent his life pushing the limits. He has completed expeditions across the Arctic circle and walked the Kokoda trail; he enjoys rock climbing, ice climbing, scuba diving and extreme skiing, and has traversed remote areas of the globe in search of adventure. Scott is in his mid-60s and, as I write, is about to do a ride from the Indian Ocean to the Pacific Ocean on a 1942 model motorbike. He has completed 113 skydives, of which none were tandem, and on one occasion his chute did not open, leaving him with the tough decision to cut away his tangled chute and engage his emergency one. Comparing this to my tandem skydiving experience made me feel like a bit of a wimp!

Scott treats life as an adventure. He explains that as a CEO you need to embrace the uncomfortable and turn towards the fear of managing uncertainty. Scott explains that not everything in business is black and white and sometimes you have to sit comfortably in the grey, find comfort in the unknown, prepare to fail, take some risks and continually learn from the experience. Creative solutions and infectious optimism are the hallmarks of his leadership. The other thing we discussed was 'change'. He explained that there are only two things that drive change in your life: one is through making a choice to change, and the other is through crisis—and unfortunately most people wait until the latter. Sadly, he's right when it comes to burnout. Most people wait until they are burnt out before they make some changes to their life, but it doesn't have to be that way. We can also make a choice, and I hope this book prompts you to do so. I really love Scott's 'matter of fact' approach to life and his adventurous nature. At the end of our chat, he left me with some sage advice from his father: 'After all is said and done, 90 per cent of the things you worry about never happen.' I couldn't agree more!

Worry creates uncertainty; uncertainty creates fear; and fear creates anxiety—it's a snowball effect. If you can catch it at the worry stage and unpack what it is that you are worried about, you may see that you are making a mountain out of a molehill or worrying about something you cannot control, or worse still, worrying about something that may not even happen. It is an absolute waste of your personal energy and resources to spend your mental energy consumed by never-ending worry and fear. It's a healthier approach to turn towards that worry and fear and ask the same two questions we asked in the previous chapter about our thoughts: 'Is it true?' and 'Is it useful?' Is what I'm worrying about even true and is it helpful for me to spend my mental energy on it?

Seeking the uncomfortable

Fear can often hold us back from realising our full potential—especially with things that are outside our comfort zone. I have been practising an exercise over the past few years that I call 'seek the uncomfortable'. I mentioned in earlier chapters that it's great to do the most demanding work tasks first up in the morning when you are at your freshest and before you get hijacked by everybody else's demands. Brian Tracy describes this beautifully in his time-management book titled *Eat That Frog*[23] when he talks about 'eating the frog' or doing the hardest task first up in the morning to eliminate procrastination and so everything else seems easier afterwards.

I really like that idea and have practised this myself, but I decided to add another layer to it. I start the day by 'seeking the uncomfortable' to help me embrace fear on a daily basis. Every morning I purposefully look for the tasks in my day that make me feel uncomfortable or provoke a bit of fear in me and I highlight them as the first thing to meet head-on. For example, it could be that tough conversation, or that hard meeting, or a tricky phone call breaking bad news, or a challenging client or anything that I don't really like doing. After circling that one thing, I then engage with that uncomfortable task and turn towards it with good intentions and a positive attitude. I must admit, it was challenging at first, but after doing it on a daily basis, it became much easier and I actually began to enjoy it because it helped me grow and develop. I was even a bit disappointed on one occasion when I looked at my day ahead and there wasn't anything too challenging to embrace.

I invite you to try this out yourself. Think of the things that make you feel a bit uncomfortable and see what you can do to meet those first up in your day instead of putting them off, because if you are anything like me, you will delay them until the afternoon and then inevitably postpone them until the following morning. When you turn towards your fears and accomplish them, it can be very rewarding and energising.

Developing a relationship with fear and trust

While trekking in the Himalayas for a few months, I had to face my fears more than once. When crossing the mountain rivers while trekking, you come across many suspended footbridges, some safer than others. They are usually suspended on wires or ropes and sway high above the valley floor. Many times they have raging rivers underneath them and they are usually very narrow, with just enough room for two people side by side. They are sometimes called 'sway bridges' because when you start walking on them they bounce and sway in all directions, and the more people that are on them, the more they bounce, which can be quite scary! You really have to put your trust in the primitive engineering of these bridges and just go for it.

I do have a fear of heights, but it's weird because it's not a problem all of the time, which is worse because it sometimes catches me by surprise. I remember the first time I had to cross a suspended bridge, I was halfway across when a team of Sherpas with laden donkeys came from the other direction onto the bridge. The bridge started bouncing and swaying so I instantly turned back around and hurried to get off the bridge and onto stable ground, scared that I'd get squashed or knocked off. I waited for ages for the bridge to be totally clear before I would cross. However, I quickly learned that there are many of these crossings among the mountain treks and eventually you have to get the courage to continue to cross them no matter what is coming towards you—otherwise you'll never get anywhere. I got so much better at it after many crossings and eventually I had zero fear whatsoever. I even managed to share bridges with yaks coming the other way!

The most confronting river crossing was not quite a suspension bridge but a flying-fox type of system with a cage made of iron and chicken wire that was suspended hundreds of metres above a raging river high up in the Himalayas. My life, and that of my travel companion, literally depended on one single cable fixed to each side of the cliffs as we sat in our chicken-wire cage while being ferried by the locals from one side to another via a series of ropes and pulleys. My heart was in my throat as we got pulled, inch by inch, over a raging river, but we eventually made it safely to the other side.

To top it off, at the end of our 18-day Himalayan trek we ran out of money from buying too many treats along the way. You see, the higher you trek in the mountains, the more expensive things are, and we probably had one too many Snickers bars and Coca-Colas along the way. We got to the end of our trek and needed to catch a bus back to Kathmandu, but we didn't have enough money for tickets. We searched through our backpacks and managed to pull together a few Nepalese rupees, which we offered the bus driver. We were motioned to follow him and he led us up a ladder to the roof of the bus. To our surprise, we were greeted up there by a few young local Nepalese boys ready for their journey. We sat on top of our backpacks and looped our hands and feet under any rails we could find as we endured the nerve-wracking six-hour ride all the way back to Kathmandu. Trust, trust, trust is all we could do!

All of these experiences gave me the confidence to constantly turn towards my fears and embrace them as best I could. Like anything, the more you expose yourself to uncomfortable situations, the more you condition yourself to develop trust in yourself and your capabilities. Sometimes when we are feeling burnt out, stressed or anxious we lose that sense of trust in our capacity and capabilities and we might avoid certain challenging situations. However, the more you expose yourself to fear and 'being comfortable with being uncomfortable', the more you can embrace the full experience of life.

On the other side of fear is trust

A fear mindset inhibits you from truly living the life you want. The fear of taking risks, the fear of failing and the fear of change can stop you moving forward. I am not a career coach, but very often I see clients who are feeling 'stuck' in their career or life because they are simply too scared to take that next big leap. This is understandable because any significant change in life is usually scary, but once you eliminate the fears and build trust instead, you are ready to progress forward with positive momentum. I was coaching Jean, a corporate executive who had spent the previous 10 years advancing her career to managing director of a medium-sized logistics company. Although she enjoyed her job and her team, she did not feel fulfilled and, in her words, she felt 'comfortably stuck'. She said she was feeling a bit burnt out and lacked the drive to keep going for another 10 years in this type of role. She discovered her true passion was to help other professional women to manage their careers while bringing up a family (she was a proud mother of three herself) and she really wanted to open her own coaching business, but she was too scared to give up the financial security she had in her job.

After some sessions in establishing trust and working out a sensible transition plan, Jean finally made the courageous move. She thought she would start it as a side business initially while still working, but within months she was so busy and successful in her coaching business that she invested herself in it full time. Her passion and drive accelerated her rapid growth and she has not turned back since. She now laughs at herself when she thinks of what she was afraid of. With trust anything is possible!

Flipping your fears

Making any big change in life is scary, but you need to truly trust yourself, trust your capabilities, trust your instincts, trust your decisions, trust your support network and go for it. Sometimes it's useful to think of what would be the worst-case scenario if you gave something a shot, and if it doesn't work out, can you deal with that? It's also beneficial to break down what it is that you are scared of so you can turn towards it and understand it better.

Another great exercise is to 'flip your fears' into trust. Let's say you are going for a job interview and you fear inadequacy. You might think something like, *I'm not good enough,* or *I'm not ready*. You can flip that thought and reassure yourself with expressions like, 'I am good enough and I am ready. I trust that I have all the knowledge and skills that I need and I will also learn new skills along the way.' This is a healthier mindset and approach for turning your fears into positive actions and validating to yourself that you've got what it takes to succeed in life.

We can use this approach for all of the basic human fears we looked at earlier in this chapter. You can see this approach at work in table 6.1.

Table 6.1 examples of flipping your fears to trust

Basic fear	You might say something like ...	Flip it to ...
Fear of inadequacy	I'm scared I'm not good enough.	I trust that I have all of the skills and knowledge I need.
Fear of rejection	I'm scared they won't accept me. (e.g. a relationship)	I trust that I will put my best foot forward and that's the best I can do.
Fear of uncertainty	I'm scared of the unknown and I don't know what will happen.	I embrace the unknown and trust that it will all work out.
Fear of change	I'm scared of making this move.	I trust that this move is going to be amazing.
Fear of missing out (FOMO)	I'm scared of missing out on something.	I trust that if it's important (to me) I'll find out about it.
Fear of being judged	I'm scared of not being liked.	I trust that they will like me just as I am.

Basic fear	You might say something like ...	Flip it to ...
Fear of losing control	I'm scared of not coping and losing control.	I trust that I will have the resources I need, and I also accept that some things are out of my control.
Fear of being hurt, (e.g. love/loss)	I'm scared of being hurt or let down.	I trust I'm worthy of love and I'll just be my genuine self.
Fear of failure	I'm scared of failing.	I trust that all will go well and if it doesn't go to plan, I will learn from that experience.

This exercise is a great way to flip your fears to trust. You can dive deeper into this exercise yourself in the practice template at the end of this chapter. The goal is to identify the main fear or the limiting belief, put it into a sentence starting with 'I'm scared...' and flip it into a positive statement starting with 'I trust that...'

Imposter syndrome and limiting beliefs

You may have heard the term 'imposter syndrome'[24], where you have a sense of self-doubt about your competency, your skills and your accomplishments. You might feel like an imposter and that you have only made it this far out of luck or faking your way there, and maybe one day somebody will find you out. For example, say you have just entered a leadership role through a series of promotions, but you believe you are not good enough for this role and you don't really have what it takes. You doubt your capability as a leader and worry that someday you will be exposed.

While limiting beliefs are a set of false beliefs that can stop you from pursuing your goals or your big dreams, many of them stem from fear, as we have discussed previously, and they can keep you in a holding pattern that prevents you from achieving greatness in your life. You might say things like:

- o I'm not good enough

- o I'm not smart enough

- o I'm not old enough

- o I'm too old

- o I'm not ready yet.

Sometimes we do not verbalise these phrases but we think them and this stops us from taking positive action. There are a variety of factors that create your limiting beliefs. They can stem from your upbringing or through certain conditioning at different stages of your life. A story that illustrates this perfectly was shared with me by an elephant trainer in Chang Mai, far north Thailand. He explained that when elephants are babies, they restrict them by attaching a thin piece of rope fixed to a peg in the ground to the little elephant's ankle. The elephant learns that it is limited to that area. As the elephant grows in weight and size, it still believes it is limited by the thin piece of rope, even though it could easily break it, so it won't even try.

... when you identify your limiting beliefs and break through them you can create anything you want in life.

Ask yourself if you have any limiting beliefs that are holding you back from realising your dreams. (The exercise at the end of this chapter will help you with this.)

Sometimes all you need to do is take that first step! When you gently turn towards your fear, you can meet it head on and have an understanding of what's creating that fear. You can then respond to it logically and mindfully. Furthermore, when you identify your limiting beliefs and break through them you can create anything you want in life. The choices are virtually limitless. I have learned that with trust and belief you will always have the right response, take the right action and use the resources inside of you just when you need them for any given situation—not before, not after, but in the moment. This belief has served me well and I'm confident it will help you too.

Here are some exercises to 'flip your fears' and break some of those limiting beliefs. Let's take some positive steps towards living your best life!

Fear-busting and trust practices

Exercise 1: Flip your fears

As we saw in table 6.1, the first exercise is to turn towards any fears you may have and define them in the first column, write a possible thought or something you might say based on this fear in the second column, and in the third column, flip the fear into a positive statement. You can do this any time you feel afraid to take a step forward or have a big decision to make or if you just need to pluck up the courage to do something.

Note: if you are having trouble defining the basic fear (in column one 1) you might want to do the second and third columns first. This may give you the clarity to determine what the basic fear is.

Basic fear	You might say something like ...	Flip it to ...
Example *Fear of inadequacy*	*I'm scared I'm not good enough.*	*I trust that I have all of the skills and knowledge I need.*
Fear of	I'm scared ...	I trust that ...
Fear of	I'm scared ...	I trust that ...
Fear of	I'm scared ...	I trust that ...

Exercise 2: Limiting beliefs

This exercise will help you understand some of the limiting beliefs that might be holding you back.

Write one limiting belief that might be holding you back. For example, 'I'm not smart enough'.

_____

Do you have any supporting evidence that this is 100 per cent true?

_____

How does this belief hinder and limit you?

_____

_____

If you broke this belief, how different would your life be?

_____

_____

Now let's reverse this belief. Write a positive statement or an empowering belief (e.g. instead of 'I'm not smart enough', say 'I am smart enough').

_____

_____

How does this new belief make you feel? What possibilities does this open for you? What evidence do you have to support this new belief and mindset?

_____

_____

_____

Note: If you would prefer not to write in the book, download a free accompanying workbook from **www.melocalarco.com**.

CHAPTER 7

ON PURPOSE AND PERSEVERANCE

I know this might sound idealistic, but my personal purpose and mission in life is to leave the world a better place than I found it. If I can help make somebody healthy or happy who can then share this with somebody else, the ripple effect will spread far and wide. This my deepest internal motivator and why I passionately and purposefully love doing the work I do.

Sometimes life can be challenging, and we might lose sight of our vision or we get caught up in the daily grind and lose motivation. This is where a degree of perseverance and 'never giving up' can really help. In this chapter I'd like to share a few different stories on purpose and perseverance as well as give you some tips to help you keep moving positively and purposefully through life. We will discuss ways to align with your purpose and values, as well as ways to adopt a positive, growth mindset so you can develop your innate ability to grow from challenging situations.

Pygmy village, Cameroon

One of my biggest goals while travelling is to share joy with the children of the world. This aligns with my mission of leaving the world a better place than I found it. When I am travelling, you will always find me among children, playing all sorts of games and having fun. There is nothing more welcoming than arriving in a new village or town and being followed by a string of curious young children smiling and chatting with you in their local language. My fellow travellers would always joke, 'If you can't find Melo, just look for a group of kids huddled together laughing and he will be the one right in the middle of them.' Whether it is approaching shy, war-torn kids in Uganda, playing street cricket in India, teaching English in China or just learning local games from the indigenous children of the world, it gives me great joy to be among them.

One experience I will never forget is spending time with a remote Pygmy tribe deep in the jungles of Cameroon. It was during an arduous hike through impenetrable forest. The landscape totally crushed the romantic images of jungles that you see in movies. There was nothing romantic about this jungle trek at all: it was horribly humid, there were annoyingly itchy biting insects everywhere and every thorn or spiky bush grabbed hold of my clothes. After many hours of antagonising jungle bashing, I and some fellow travellers arrived in a remote Pygmy village deep in the impenetrable forests. This tribe had rarely been visited by Western people due to its remoteness and I was excited to be there. As we arrived at a clearing containing small huts, we offered the chief and elders some gifts so we could stay in their village for the night, and they gratefully accepted.

The moment I arrived, a young boy named Limbau jumped onto my shoulders like a little monkey. He remained with me for the next 24 hours, never leaving my side. He taught me how to light fires to dispel rows of giant stinging ants, which can apparently kill a small animal. He taught me how to dance along to the local music and he shared some fun games using sticks and stones with me and his friends. It was an amazing exchange considering there was no common language—just innocent smiles and laughter. The whole experience of being among this remote Pygmy tribe was quite amazing, from hunting and dancing, to cooking, eating and just immersing myself in the whole experience.

One of the most magical moments was when Limbau, still perched on my shoulders, directed me to a waterhole, with his young friends joining us. I believe it was a secret water source and I'm not sure he was supposed to take me there. As far as I could gather, Limbau was the chief's son, so he had a few special rights. It also seemed that no girls were permitted to enter this sacred spot. With Limbau leading from my shoulders, we quietly ventured along a small path and eventually arrived at the waterhole. I was astounded by what I saw. This was the idyllic jungle scene that I had imagined from the movies: it was like something out of the *Deep Forest* soundtrack. The best landscapers in the world could not have matched this scene. There was a natural high wall of hard clay earth surrounding a deep, clear water pond surrounded by lush green foliage, creating a natural swimming pool. I was overcome by the natural beauty of this place. There were thousands of butterflies moving about the foliage and while I stood awestruck by the scene, I suddenly felt my strong little friends pick me up—like worker ants picking up a leaf—and throw me into the refreshingly clean water. For the next hour or so, we splashed and played in the water and I felt a million miles away from any civilised world. It was pure joy!

Yes, the jungle trek was confronting and hard work, and I got some terrible bites and stings along the way, but with some perseverance I reached our destination and all of that was forgotten the moment Limbau jumped on my shoulders. I felt an instant alignment to my goals, purpose and mission and it reminded me why I had embarked on this great travelling adventure in the first place!

Somewhere in Benin

Thud, thud, thud, thud! It sounded like a helicopter had landed on the roof, awakening me with such a startle that I was thrust upright in the hotel room bed. The sound echoed loudly in the corners of the room and simultaneously throbbed profusely inside my head. Pushing through the intense, throbbing pain and piercing sound, I looked up to see the ceiling fan thudding. The whirring blades sent vibrating pain and shivers through my head and body as I tried to orient myself.

My sheets were drenched with sweat as my body convulsed violently in pain. I alternated from uncontrollably shivering with cold, with my teeth chattering, to being on fire, with my forehead burning with fever. The only relief I felt from the pain in my head was when a stabbing pain in my stomach took the focus from my head to my belly area. It felt like a serrated knife was hacking its way through my intestines, crippling me with pain. This was without a doubt the most excruciating fever I had ever experienced!

The bright red digits of the alarm clock read 3:10 am. Even the red lights hurt my throbbing head as I tried to dim them. I think I must have slept for about 20 minutes because I knew I went to the bathroom at 2:50 am, and before that at 2:27 am. I felt the need to vomit again, my body contracting and convulsing. Not that I had anything left inside of me because I had been emptying my body for the past 20 hours.

I had worked out where I was—in a basic hotel room somewhere in Benin—because my lovely travelling companion, Kila, had put me up in a room with a fan so that I didn't have to sleep in my tent for a few days and could recover. She dabbed my forehead occasionally with a wet flannel, which momentarily relieved some of the pain, but the relief was only temporary. My hotel room felt, and looked, like a prison cell: there were no pictures on the dirty walls, and there was one tiny window with broken latches covered by a grimy curtain. The only thing that differentiated this room from a prison cell was the open door to the outside world, which let in a bit of fresh air occasionally.

I knew I was in trouble when Hilmar—the Icelandic friend (and doctor) we were travelling with—said, 'You don't look great. You look orange and you might need to get to a hospital.' The previous two or three days were a bit of a blur, but I did remember going in a bush taxi to the closest thing that resembled a hospital in rural Africa and getting a blood test, which confirmed what we all suspected...malaria! Not just your everyday malaria, but a very strong strain that was killing the locals, according to the hospital doctor. I had been taking antimalarial tablets weekly, but obviously the mosquito that had bitten me didn't care too much about that, rendering me with a bad, bad case of malaria.

The next few days were a rollercoaster ride of rising body temperatures of 42+ degrees, stabbing stomach pains, violent shivers, severe muscle ache, vomiting bile, vivid hallucinations, pounding headaches, and my skin and eyes turning a deeper shade of yellow to orange by the hour. I could tell by the shocked reaction on people's faces when they saw me that I did not look good. Some people recommended I should fly home to Australia or anywhere in the civilised Western world to get treated and I could tell by their expressions that they were genuinely concerned. Other people said I should get treated locally as the locals would have better knowledge of specific malarial strains prevalent in the area and which treatments were working best for each particular strain. I needed to make a decision fast.

I really didn't know what to do. For a brief moment I even thought death might be the best outcome because I was in such intense pain and feeling so weak. In my weakest moment I truly wasn't sure if I had the strength to make it and I definitely didn't have the energy to be enduring a long-haul international flight to find treatment. I remember thinking to myself I'd probably die in the air and that wouldn't be a good place to die. In the days that followed I believe I lost 5 to 10 kilograms of muscle mass. I was jaundiced, weak and it took all of my strength just to stand upright before having to sit or lie down again.

How am I going to persevere? I thought to myself. Then I convinced myself, I'm not a quitter and I never have been!

In my fragile state I finally made the decision to stay in Benin and get treated locally. Partly because I felt that 'local knowledge' for this particular strain was better than some tropical disease unit thousands of miles away, and to be perfectly honest, I did not have the energy to stand, let alone travel for 20 hours on an international flight.

The next few days, I vaguely remember travelling in more bush taxis to various local clinics and makeshift hospitals, campground first-aid tents and anything that resembled a medical centre. Somehow, through fate, I met a couple of young Canadian doctors/researchers who were trialling a drug that was working on my particular strain of malaria and they asked if I was interested in trying this new drug. It was a combination of synthetic and natural ingredients that hadn't been released to the market as yet but was getting good trial results in the local area. It was a bit of a risk, but looking in the mirror and seeing my gaunt yellow face with no white left in my eyes—only bloodshot red and orange—the decision was easy. 'What have I got to lose?' I said, and I started taking the drug cocktail immediately.

It was a course of 10 days in total with a dosage of 10 pills one day and then nine, then eight, and so on. To this day, I'm not sure exactly what was in the pills, but I recall the Canadians showing me some pharmaceutical drawings that had something to do with Artesunate and Mefloquine—or something like that. The truth be told, it didn't matter because day by day I started feeling better and by about day 3

I was able to keep some plain rice down without vomiting. It took all of my strength to get dressed and do simple things without breaking into a sweat and needing to lie down again, but every day I felt marginally better and was able to eat and drink a bit more.

Eventually, after about 10 days, I came back to some semblance of a functioning person again and was able to do a little more each day. My orange skin faded to light yellow and I could begin to see the white in my eyes again, and was able to continue my journey through central Africa. I am eternally grateful for the people who looked after me through this, especially my lovely Swiss companion (who is now my beautiful wife, by the way), Doctor Hilmar and the Canadian doctors for being in the right place at the right time. This definitely taught me some major lessons in life: to persevere, no matter what life throws at you, to have the courage to make big decisions and trust in the people around you, and that you will always have the means to get through anything with some perseverance and purpose.

Perseverance and purpose served me well throughout my travels and continue to guide me in my personal and professional life today.

Life lesson: Purpose and perseverance

When you align with your purpose and vision you can stay motivated and energised to persevere towards your goals no matter how challenging life gets.

Climbing that mountain

Perseverance is the continued effort to achieve something despite the obstacles or challenges you face along the way. It is a skill you can develop to continually stay focused on your goal and work diligently towards it, no matter how difficult or demanding it is. Usually, the sense of achievement you feel when you reach the

Perseverance is the continued effort to achieve something despite the obstacles or challenges you face along the way.

goal far outweighs the stress and load of getting there. Take, for example, mountain climbing: it can be physically and mentally demanding and painful reaching the peak, but once you stand there and admire the view and your sense of achievement, all of the pain subsides. Similarly, when undertaking a big project at work, it may be stressful and tiresome getting to the end point, but completing the project is rewarding.

On my first big 18-day trek in the Himalayas, I had horrible altitude sickness at just 3200 metres — and the highest pass I needed to cross was 5416 metres. How was I supposed to manage that? However, day by day I persevered, one step at a time. I must admit it was tough and very demanding on my body and my mind, but I eventually made it to the top of the pass. The feeling I had sitting among the colourful prayer flags on Thorung La at 5416 metres was exhilarating as I gazed out to the surrounding peaks. It was worth every ounce of effort. I can only imagine how the true mountaineers feel when they scale Everest, K2 and the world's highest peaks.

We all have our own mountains to climb and challenges to overcome, but if you approach them one step at a time and trust that you will have the resources you need, everything is possible. Even if it seems impossible at the time, or overwhelmingly difficult, remind yourself you have gone through tough times and difficult situations before and you will always pull through. Sometimes we just need to break down big, overwhelming tasks into smaller goals and milestones so we feel we are working towards smaller manageable targets. Couple this with the right amount of perseverance and purpose and you can achieve absolutely anything.

Humans like progress

When life seems overwhelming or you are feeling fatigued or burnt out everything might feel like a difficult task, as though you are not progressing forward in life. You might feel like you are just 'spinning the wheels' and not going anywhere. I do know one thing, from coaching hundreds of high-performing individuals: that humans like progress. It is a basic human need, and if you don't feel like you are moving forward you can get frustrated and lose momentum in life.

Progress is an innate biological and psychological need that drives a child from crawling to walking, from dependence to independence, from education to career, and so on. All through life we have the innate desire to constantly grow, develop, evolve and expand our sense of being. If we are not doing this, we are doing the

> **All through life we have the innate desire to constantly grow, develop, evolve and expand our sense of being.**

opposite—that is, we are stagnant, shrinking and contracting— which gives us feelings of worthlessness or hopelessness. It doesn't matter how big or small the goal is, as long as we are working towards something, we feel a sense of purposefulness and direction. I understand when you are feeling out of balance or exhausted that the last thing you want to do is set yourself more tasks and goals, but this is the one thing that will help you take action and move forward.

One of the hardest hit industries during the years of the COVID-19 pandemic was the travel industry because all local and international travel was instantly brought to a standstill. I asked Karsten Horne, CEO of Reho Travel, what kept him going and how he persevered through the toughest of times. He explained that although it was hard and frustrating, he managed to keep a positive mindset by focusing on things that were in his control. He had no control over government decisions, lockdowns or the severe travel restrictions, so he chose not to put his focus on the things he could not control. Instead, he found ways to do things that were within his control. He spent his time being creative with his thousands of hours of travel video footage, developing new business ventures and ideas, looking after his health and renovating his house. He felt that although travel was restricted, he was progressing towards something and this kept him moving forward with perseverance and purpose. Karsten is also a marathon runner so he is no stranger to persevering when times get tough physically and mentally.

To help you find balance in your life, set positive intentions and goals so that you feel you are constantly progressing and achieving. This does not mean you have to push yourself towards further fatigue and burnout. Set realistic milestones and diligently persevere towards them with a sense of purpose. Some simple, achievable goals could be:

- o to walk every morning for 45 minutes
- o to start a new project or hobby
- o to go away for a family weekend
- o to join a sporting or community club
- o to be more social and catch up more with friends
- o to study or learn something new.

The sky is the limit... What are you thinking of doing?

Never give up on your dreams

One of my most inspiring clients and friends is young Tess Lloyd, a 27-year-old Olympic athlete (sailing) who shared her moving story about perseverance, resilience and purpose with me. Ever since seeing Cathy Freeman win gold in the 2000 Olympics[25], Tess—who was just five years old at the time—knew she wanted to one day represent Australia as an Olympic athlete. She found her passion for sailing at a young age and worked very hard to improve her skills while going through her schooling years.

Unfortunately, at 16 years of age, during a national sailing competition in Queensland, Australia, Tess was involved in a most unfortunate 'freak' accident where she was hit in the side of the head by a windsurfer. (It was unusual circumstances in that the two races—windsurfers and 29ers sailing boats—were combined into one race.) The weather conditions were atrocious, and Tess was left unconscious in her sailing vessel with her head face-down in the water. Her friend lifted her out of the water and signalled for help. It took some time before anyone realised the severity of the incident because it was common for sailing boats to capsize during races, so the rescue vessels did not respond immediately, so Tess was left injured and bleeding for a while before she could get help.

In the ambulance on the way to the hospital, the paramedics called for an emergency doctor to come on board because she was in a life-and-death situation. Once in the hospital, x-rays revealed a fractured skull, which expanded into her brain and was causing all sorts of complications. Thankfully the surgeons managed to save Tess and put a plate with eight screws in her head. She was then put into an induced coma for three weeks. When Tess came out of the coma, the doctors tactfully warned her parents that she might not be able to walk and talk as she could before, and that her memory and balance had been severely impaired.

Tess persevered through more than two painstaking years of hard work, learning to read, speak and write proficiently again. She worked hard on reclaiming her memory and received extensive physiotherapy for her balance. She did all of this while struggling through her final year of high school which she did over a period of two years. Six months later, Tess was back in the boat. This is where she felt most comfortable and she still wanted to fulfil her childhood dream. She trained her body and mind to get stronger and worked tirelessly to rebuild her sailing skills because she had her sights on the 2016 Rio Olympics.

After three years of diligent training, she received the upsetting news that she hadn't qualified for the Rio Olympics, but Tess didn't give up. Next, she set her sights on the 2020 Tokyo Olympics and trained even harder to make the grade. Yes! She and her sailing companion, Jaime, were accepted and they were so excited! This meant more years of disciplined training routines and doing the best she could to represent Australia in 2020. Months before the event, COVID-19 put a stop to the world, and the Olympics were postponed for a year. Dealing with all of the uncertainty, anxiety and disappointment, Tess persevered and kept training hard for another year. They lost their coach due to a string of unforeseen circumstances and got a last-minute replacement but they finally made it to the Tokyo Olympics in 2021.

Her childhood dream became a reality as she and Jaime raced their 49er FX sailing boat to represent Australia. It was an amazing experience and although they didn't win any medals, they were happy with how they performed. I explained to Tess on one of our virtual coaching sessions that I consider her a gold medallist just for being there after all that she had gone through over the previous 10 years. A gold medal in perseverance in my eyes! At the time of writing, Tess has her sights on the Paris Olympics in 2024. Go Tess!

Aligning with purpose

Could you run a 42-kilometre marathon tomorrow?

This is something I jokingly ask in one of my corporate seminars. I open with the question, 'Who could run a full 42-kilometre marathon tomorrow morning starting at 6 am?' As you can imagine, nobody puts up their hand— though there may be an exception if there is a marathon runner in the room.

> **Creating a vision and aligning with your purpose is the cornerstone to keeping you balanced and grounded.**

Then I add some purpose to the question. I ask the group to imagine that someone they love dearly has a horrible sickness and that at the end of the marathon there is a magic serum that will miraculously make them better. 'Now who can run a 42-kilometre marathon tomorrow morning starting at 6 am?' and every single hand goes up, regardless of their fitness level, because I have added a deep purpose to the mission.

Creating a vision and aligning with your purpose is the cornerstone to keeping you balanced and grounded. It doesn't matter how big or small your vision is. As long as it aligns with your values and is true to what you believe in, it is your guiding light to staying on track when life gets challenging. Purpose can make you ask some of life's big contemplative questions, such as:

o   Why am I here?

o   Who am I?

o   What do I want in life?

o   Where do I belong?

o   What fulfils me?

These are all very good questions to ask yourself. But purpose doesn't always have to be the big questions or visions; it can also be how you go about your everyday life. Purpose can guide your life decisions, give you clarity, shape your goals and give you a sense of clear direction. For some people purpose can be very closely related to their work. For others, their purpose may be separate from their work—for example, it may be in relation to their family. Purpose is personal, no matter how big or small it is.

Purpose is as unique as your fingerprint. What you value most and what you identify as your direction may be vastly different from that of the people around you—this is what makes us unique individuals. True purpose is about valuing your own skills or gifts and sharing those with the world in some way. It may be solving someone's problem, playing music for someone, bringing joy to someone's life, or simply being there for a friend or your family.

True purpose is about valuing your own skills or gifts and sharing those with the world in some way.

John Rowland, the IT executive we met in chapter 5, clearly articulated to me that his deeper purpose in life is his responsibility to his family. His family is the highest in his hierarchy of values, and being successful at work gives him the means to provide for his family as best he can. He strives for excellence at work and admits he does work long hours from time to time. But underneath it all is his sense of purpose, which continues to drive him to achieve his goals. He is very clear on his 'why' and that is how he manages to maintain balance in his life and work.

A busy accountant I work with once asked me jokingly, 'How can I find purpose in accounting and bookkeeping? It's so mundane!' However, once he discovered he likes helping people solve problems, he realised that helping people (with their finances) was part of his purpose and that made him feel good. He also similarly knew it was a way to fulfil another deeper purpose of providing for his young family, which was very important to him.

It doesn't have to change the world, just your world

Your purpose does not have to be the biggest mission on the planet, like bringing about peace on earth. It also doesn't need to be your job. It may be as simple as waking up in the morning to make a healthy breakfast for your family; or seeking happiness every day. The key element of purpose is alignment: when you are aligned with your values and your 'reason for being', you will feel connection and contribution to the world around you.

Many people I have spoken to who experienced burnout felt directionless and purposeless and did not have any reason to get out of bed in the morning. The Japanese concept of *Ikigai* translates roughly to 'your reason for being' or 'your reason for waking up in the morning'. *Iki* means 'life', and *gai* describes value or worth. It's quite a beautiful concept in that it explores finding something you are passionate about and creating a mission around it, which may (or may not) become your vocation. You share it with the world, but at the very centre of it all is your *Ikigai*, your reason for being.

Intrinsic rather than extrinsic motivators

Many people struggle to find balance when they are misaligned with their purpose or aren't even sure what it is in the first place. I have coached many executives and high achievers who feel they will be happy when they get that new promotion or pay rise, or a company car, or they become a general manager, only to find that when they get there, they are still unhappy. When you constantly chase the next thing to be happy, it may bring short-term happiness. Before long, though, you will be on the hunt for the next big thing to make you happier. These external rewards are known as 'extrinsic motivators' and although they can motivate you to strive higher and drive you towards a goal, they are only temporary. Take the example of a pay rise or bonus: if you are only chasing the pay rise, how much will ever be enough? It's great to be incentivised to work harder in the short term but that may not motivate you in the long run.

The opposite of this is to be 'intrinsically motivated': to enjoy the work you are doing with a clear sense of purpose on what motivates you from the inside. It's is about discovering what motivates you from the inside despite your external rewards. Figure 7.1 describes the difference between extrinsic and intrinsic motivators.

Extrinsic motivators	Intrinsic motivators
○ Driven by external factors ○ Motivated by money ○ Focused on end result ○ Fixed mindset ○ Needs constant validation and support	○ Driven from within ○ Motivated by purpose ○ Enjoyable process ○ Growth mindset ○ Works with more autonomy and mastery

Figure 7.1 extrinsic vs intrinsic motivators

One of my clients, James, was dissatisfied with his role in middle management, so he worked as hard as he could to get a role as a general manager, even to the detriment of his own health. It was at this stage that I met him: he was suffering from anxiety; he was unhealthy, unhappy and chronically stressed, but he still thought in his mind that this would all be resolved when he moved up to the next rank in the company.

Then he discovered that if he wasn't happy now, how would this change when he became the general manager? If anything, there would be more responsibility, more stress and more pressure, which may not be so motivating.

We did some work around values, purpose and defining what success meant to him and he was surprised that the definition of success was far from what he was chasing. Once James established that it wasn't the external factors that would make him happy, but rather his internal 'reason for being', his whole world changed. He established a clear sense of purpose and direction and realised that intrinsic motivators are far more important than any external rewards. He also regained balance in other areas of his life that had been neglected in his race to the top. His family life improved, his relationships improved, and he even had time to go out with his friends more, which brought him great joy.

The 'five whys'

One of my favourite coaching exercises can be useful for finding a fast way to get to the bottom of things and find purpose. It's called the 'five whys' technique and I'd like to share it with you. This technique was developed by Sakichi Toyoda—a Japanese industrialist, inventor and founder of Toyota Industries—in the 1930s, and was popularised in the 1970s. Toyota still uses the technique to solve problems today. I have used this with many clients and I also use it on myself as a self-coaching technique when I'm confused or need some clarity with a decision-making process. As the name suggests, you ask the question 'Why?' five times to find out what's behind your thinking regarding a particular issue. Many people are surprised that by the time they get to the fifth question, their response is far different from what they initially thought.

I'll share an example here so that it makes more sense. Let's imagine somebody wants to be the general manager of a large company:

Question 1: Why is it important for you to be a
general manager?
Response: So I am recognised for the hard work
I am doing.

Question 2: Why is it important for you to be recognised for your hard work?

Response: So I have some senior status and am acknowledged for my contribution to the company.

Question 3: Why is it important to be acknowledged for how you contribute to the company and have senior status?

Response: So I have more responsibility and am financially rewarded for my efforts.

Question 4: Why is it important for you to be financially rewarded for your efforts?

Response: So I can have financial security.

Question 5: Why is it important to have financial security?

Response: So I can provide for my family and give my children the best education.

Ideally, by the time you get to the fifth question, you have a response that aligns with your values. In the example above, family and education are high values for this person. Sometimes you might only need three 'whys' to get to the solution, or sometimes you may need more than five, but you will know you have got there because it will feel right. It's a great way to unpack a solution and get to the real meaning of why something is important to you. Give it a try at the end of this chapter!

Knowing your values

Staying intrinsically motivated and realigning with your purpose also comes down to knowing your core values. When we lose alignment with our core values, we may lose direction and consequently lose balance in life. Most people I ask about core values struggle to come up with their top three values in life. Companies see the great importance of defining their core business values and we should also be clear on defining our personal core values.

Personal values are individual beliefs and morals that guide your behaviours and differentiate right from wrong. They are your personal code of conduct and they highlight what you stand for. They are important because they guide your decisions, give you direction, connect you with others and align you

> **Personal values are individual beliefs and morals that guide your behaviours and differentiate right from wrong.**

with your purpose. Research shows that defining your values and understanding what makes a meaningful life are very valuable skills that can help you manage stress, navigate challenges and support your mental health[26]. When we are clear on our values, our ability to make better decisions and choices in life is improved.

Our values are influenced by and formed at different stages in our life:

o   At the age of 1–7 years we are predominantly influenced by our parents (or guardians).

o   At the age of 8–13 years we are mostly guided by teachers, friends, heroes (sports stars, celebrities, TV characters and music stars).

o   At the age of 14–20 years we are influenced by close friends, university peers, colleagues, 'fitting in' and self-discovery.

o   From 21 to adulthood our core values are established, but these may vary depending on different phases in life, e.g. career phase, parent phase.

When you make values-based decisions, they are always the right ones and you feel confident to stand up for your beliefs. If something does not sit well with you because it goes against your values, it may be worth expressing that and letting people know where you stand. When we connect with people based on our values, we make a much deeper connection because we can understand each other on a deeper level. However, everyone has different core values, and we won't always see eye to eye on everything. That's fine, as long as we openly communicate this in a non-judgemental way.

Getting to know your values

It is important to establish what your top three to five values are as they guide every behaviour and everything you act upon with a sense of clear purpose. A good warm-up exercise to help you narrow this down is to think about the key assets and values that you admire in the people around you. This could be anyone from your family, friends, bosses, CEOs, sporting celebrities, global leaders and absolutely anyone you have respect for and admire. Ask yourself:

o   What is it you like about them?

o   Why do you align with them?

o   What is it they stand for?

o   What do you think their highest value is?

Another good exercise that could be quite interesting is to ask somebody what they think your top three values are. Or have some fun and simply ask them to describe you in three words. You may be surprised by their response.

It's amazing how developing a sense of purpose, persevering towards your goals and knowing your values can change your world.

In the following practices section, you will find a handy exercise to help you refine your top three values.

Purpose and perseverance practices

Now that we've explored the importance of purpose and perseverance in your life, let's find out your five 'whys' and define your values.

Practice 1: The 'five whys'

What I love about this exercise is its simplicity and the depth you can get from such a short activity. Here's how it goes.

- *Step 1:* Think of a goal or something that you are trying to decide on. For example, starting your own business.

- *Step 2:* Turn it into a question by opening with 'Why is it important to...?'

  For example: Why is it important to start my own business?

  An example response could be: To choose my own hours and not have a boss.

  Turn this into the next question: Why is it important to run my own business and choose my own hours?

- *Step 3:* Continue this process five times, always turning the response back into a question by starting with 'Why is it important to...?'

- *Step 4:* Reflect on the final response and see how it aligns with your values and purpose.

Practice 2: Defining your top three values

- *Step 1:* First of all, write a list of about 20 values—words that mean something to you. For example, honest, caring, integral, approachable, fun, experience, direct, and so on. If you get stuck, you can Google '200 values' and choose something from that list.

○ *Step 2:* Then circle or group similar ones. For example, kindness and compassion, or strength and courage. Next, see if you can narrow it down to about 10 values.

○ *Step 3:* Now be totally ruthless and try to narrow it down to just three or five values. This doesn't mean the others are not meaningful to you, but these top three are non-negotiable.

○ *Step 4:* Write them down and clearly define what they mean to you personally.

Lastly, take those top three to five values and embody them as best you can. Let them be your guide to making clear decisions and acting upon the values that align with you.

Have fun!

CHAPTER 8

ON GRATITUDE AND COMPASSION

To regain balance in your life, one of the most powerful practices you can adopt is an attitude of gratitude. Practising gratitude simply means noticing and appreciating many of the good things that surround you in your life as opposed to all of the 'not so good' things. Ultimately, we all have a choice and it us up to us to decide what we tune into in our life. This not only affects our psychology but also our physiology. When we focus on the stress and negativity in our life our body releases stress chemicals. The opposite is true when we practise gratitude: our bodies release 'feel-good' chemicals and hormones. I know what I'd rather have swirling around in my body—how about you? Once you start tuning in to the goodness that surrounds you every day, it can have enormous wellbeing benefits, including boosting your physical and mental health, improving your relationships and your self-esteem, and many more benefits, which we will discuss in this chapter.

> To regain balance in your life, one of the most powerful practices you can adopt is an attitude of gratitude.

Masai Mara, Kenya

How did I end up here? I can't breathe. I feel like I'm suffocating from the smoke and I'm trapped inside a small home, in the Masai Mara.

While travelling through the Mara national game reserve, a very kind Masai family offered me their bed for the night in their 'manyatta', which is a traditional Masai family home made from sticks, clay and cow dung. I've slept in some horrendous beds throughout my travels, from rock-hard floors, to soft lumpy mattresses and everything in between, but I must say this has to be the worst bed I have ever slept in. It's alive!

As I laid my head down on the bed made of sticks, twigs, animal hide and other bush materials, I could hear the movement of insects beneath me. It sounded like termites gnawing or a colony of bugs working, and I felt the occasional bite on my legs. How could I possibly get any sleep? It felt like bugs were crawling all over my skin and the sound of gnawing intensified in my ears as the night went on. The smoke from the fire keeping us warm was suffocating me. Every time I inhaled, I burnt my nostrils; my mouth was parched; and my throat was choking closed. I managed to find a small hole in the cow-dung wall near my bed and I literally put my mouth against it to draw in the fresh, cold air from outside. I wished I had a straw so I could use it like a snorkel. I was choking, gasping for air and I couldn't sleep. However, I was still grateful that I was safe and warm because it was freezing outside.

I wanted to go outside to get some fresh air for a minute, but I noticed a stick propped up against the inside of the door. I recalled a Masai warrior saying that when the male of the household was out hunting (which he was) other males would sometimes come in and take advantage of the women. I was trapped inside with a Masai mother and her five children so I persevered into the early hours of the morning.

Exhausted, I finally started to drift off to sleep, but then, suddenly, I heard what I thought was water gushing near my head, like somebody had turned on a tap, and I smelt the intense odour of urine permeating the smoke-filled air. It was from a big brown cow nestled up beside us. You see, the Masai often sleep with their animals inside their manyatta to keep them safe and also for warmth during the colder nights. This family home had four children, one cow, three goats, a puppy dog and of course the insect colony in my bed. There was no chance I was getting any sleep tonight as the goats bleated, the cow farted and the dog played, while the insects kept gnawing at my bed. I gave up and deliriously stayed awake all night laughing to myself at the absurd circumstances.

When morning came, I could hear the chatter in the village outside as everyone went about their morning activities. I observed the Masai mother put a log on the smouldering fire. I also noticed that the whole family, all five of them, had slept, huddled together, on a small, makeshift bed on the floor. The youngest child was not moving very much as the rest of the family started shuffling in the morning light. The mother held her limp son and tried to explain, using sign language and a few broken English words, that the child was extremely sick with life-threatening malaria. This really put things in perspective for me. The whole family had slept on the floor for me, opening up their family home and providing me with warmth, safety and comfort for the night, sacrificing their own comfort. I was eternally grateful.

This experience and many others in Africa taught me the importance of kindness, gratitude and compassion. It taught me that there are so many things we take for granted in the Western world and being grateful for the smallest things is so often overlooked. The children of Africa are grateful for the simplest home-made toys, like a stick and an old bicycle rim, which they can play with for endless hours. Meanwhile, in the West our children are complaining that they are not happy with their latest digital game and want a new one, or can't occupy themselves for longer than half an hour without being 'bored.'

I experienced many acts of kindness like this one in Africa from families and people who seemingly have nothing but will still give you everything with a smile. I learned to appreciate all things great and small, from fresh running water, having comfortable shoes and clothes to wear, choices of food to eat and endless opportunities in life.

Life lesson: Gratitude and compassion

Never take things for granted. Focus on being grateful for what you have, not what you don't have. Small acts of kindness, compassion and gratitude can positively change your world, and that of others too. The power of gratitude rests in your ability to positively change the way you view the world.

What is gratitude?

The word 'gratitude' isn't always straightforward to classify. It can be described as an attitude, an emotion, a practice, a personality, a trait or a habit. The Latin word *gratia* means grace, gratefulness or graciousness. Many derivatives of the word are related to giving and receiving, kindness, generosity, gifts and appreciation.

Gratitude is taking the time to pause and notice all the things you have around you, even the small things you might take for granted. Little things like clean running water to drink, fresh air to breathe, a place to live, warmth, your health, family and friends. Sometimes we just need to take a moment and reflect on how blessed we are to realise every day brings us some beauty and happiness. There are so many small moments that happen in the course of a day and many times we are on autopilot and we miss them or take them for granted.

This reminds me of a moment in time with a good friend of mine, Nicola Catalano (Nic), who I used to work with at a school years ago. I was out on the back oval looking at the most amazing rainbow stretching across the sky. It was the clearest rainbow I had ever seen, with its very distinct seven colours. It was quite magical, and I really wanted to share it with somebody. I went into the staff room and invited Nic outside to show her. We both stood there for a moment appreciating the beauty of this rainbow. We had both seen many rainbows before, but this one turned out to be quite special because, little did we know, this was the last rainbow that Nic would ever see. Shortly afterwards, Nic was tragically diagnosed with an aggressive brain tumour and after years of various invasive surgical interventions, she lost her sense of taste and other faculties and is now totally blind. She still has a super positive outlook on life and has shared her experiences in an inspiring book called *Can't Get You Out of My Head*[27], which captures her courage, endurance, positive outlook and sense of humour. Bless her: she expresses gratitude for everything she still has and is an inspiration by continually looking at life through a positive lens. Thanks to Nic I now always stop and take the time to experience the wonder of the natural phenomenon that is a rainbow.

> **Gratitude is taking the time to pause and notice all the things you have around you, even the small things you might take for granted.**

Think of all the things we take for granted in our day. It's not because we mean to, but sometimes we go through life on 'autopilot' and miss the good moments, or we just get too busy to stop. Children are our best teachers when it comes to slowing down and enjoying the wonders of the world—it's often we, as busy adults, who rush them through life. For example, you're walking along the beach and your child stops at every collection of shells and studies them with curiosity and a sense of wonder. You walk ahead and after some time you become impatient and say, 'Hurry up, we're going to be late!' Your mind is already on the way to the next place instead of enjoying where you are. As an adult you have seen those shells a million times before and you hardly notice them anymore, while your curious child is gratefully enjoying every single one. Sometimes we just need to slow down and 'smell the roses', as they say, to enjoy the little things in life.

Take a pause for a moment right now to look around you and reflect on what you are grateful for.

Not just 'warm and fuzzy'

Often when I mention the word 'gratitude' or 'compassion' in my corporate seminars, I notice people rolling their eyes or I get the feeling they don't think gratitude is important for a successful executive. Some people think gratitude is just 'warm and fuzzy', but there is ground-breaking science about the benefits of practising gratitude. In fact, a 2018 white paper from The Greater Good Science Centre, UC, Berkeley, summarises the evidence-based benefits of practising gratitude[28]. There are far too many to list here, but I'd like to share with you just a few science-backed reasons to adopt a gratitude practice:

o *It releases feel-good chemicals*: when you practise gratitude, kindness and compassion, your body naturally releases uplifting chemicals such as dopamine and oxytocin, which instantly make you feel good.

o *It rewires your brain positively*: the brain is continually changing—science calls this 'neuroplasticity'. We can literally rewire the positive neural pathways in the brain by practising gratitude and compassion.

- o *It decreases stress and reactivity*: when we strengthen the positive pathways and regions of the brain, we also weaken the regions associated with stress and anxiety.

- o *It improves sleep*: studies have shown that practising gratitude before going to bed helps people lower their heart rate and fall asleep more easily as well as improving the quality of sleep[29].

The reticular activating system (RAS)

Have you heard of the reticular activating system (RAS)?

It's a network of regions of the brain that mediates your perceptive awareness and acts as a filter for what your brain receives. It helps you look for the things that matter most to you based on your values, needs, goals and desires and it also looks for familiarity. Let's say you are thinking of buying a brand-new car: a bright red mini, for example, because you haven't seen too many of them around and you want something different. Just by tuning in to bright red mini cars you start noticing them more and more on the road, and then you finally buy one and you see them everywhere—they aren't so unique after all! This is your RAS tuning in to red mini cars. They were always there; the only difference is that now you have signalled to your brain to notice them more. Sound familiar?

The more you practise or experience gratitude, the more you reinforce your RAS to filter this information to you because it is important to you.

It's the same for gratitude and compassion: the more you practise, the more your RAS will notice it. You will begin to notice the cheerful person who smiles at you, or your colleague who holds the door open for you or buys you a coffee, or the nice email you get from a client, or the beautiful sunny day. The more you practise or experience gratitude, the more you reinforce your RAS to filter this information to you because it is important to you. The RAS doesn't distinguish between positive or negative thoughts: it only knows what you are giving attention to and it deems that as important, so it will notice more of that. In other words, be mindful of what you give your attention to every day. If you tune in to the negative things around you, you will notice more of them; if you tune in to gratitude and compassion you will begin to notice and appreciate all the good things that happen in your day. What would you rather give your attention to?

This was demonstrated in an interesting randomised control study where participants who were receiving psychotherapy were randomly assigned to three groups and some had to keep a journal for four weeks:

o Group A (the control group) received psychotherapy only (no journal writing).

o Group B received psychotherapy and had to express their deepest negative thoughts and feelings about stressful experiences in writing.

o Group C received psychotherapy and were asked to write letters expressing gratitude towards others (gratitude writing).

About four weeks after the study concluded, participants in group C reported significantly better mental health and wellbeing than the others and this continued for up to 12 weeks[30].

Writing down things you are a grateful for can be a powerful practice for shifting your awareness to see things in a positive light. It hardwires the brain and RAS to recognise and search for more happy moments in your day that make you feel good and releases the happy chemicals in your body. The great thing is, it's very simple and it's easy to incorporate in your life without too much effort. I will share a gratitude exercise at the end of this chapter.

Experiencing happiness

Unfortunately, when we are feeling stressed, tired and burnt out it's not always easy to appreciate what we have, and we tend to only tune in to our negative feelings and emotions, which creates more anxiety, depression or negativity. This brings us back to practising self-awareness, so that you catch these thoughts early and intervene with a practice such as breathing or turning towards your thoughts, which we learned about in previous chapters. By practising gratitude, you focus on the good things around you, which boosts your happiness and decreases the feelings of hopelessness and depression.

If you Google 'Who is the happiest person in the world?', whose name do you think pops up?

It's a French man by the name of Matthieu Ricard, a geneticist who became a Buddhist monk and is the author of many books including *Altruism and Happiness: A Guide to Developing Life's Most Important Skill*. What makes Ricard so happy? Regular meditation,

> **By practising gratitude, you focus on the good things around you, which boosts your happiness and decreases the feelings of hopelessness and depression.**

particularly on compassion and gratitude. To quantify this, Ricard was involved in an intensive study by neuroscientists at the University of Wisconsin, where 256 sensors were attached to his scalp[31]. When he meditated on attitudes of kindness, gratitude and compassion towards others, areas of his brain lit up, particularly the left prefrontal cortex, which is associated with positivity and happiness. He also shocked researchers by demonstrating abnormally high levels of gamma wave activity, something that had never been recorded before in scientific literature. Gamma activity is linked to higher consciousness, attention, peak performance, learning and memory. This does not mean you need the dedication of a monk to experience happiness—just a regular meditation and gratitude practice can give you great benefits. In Ricard's words, 'Anyone can be the happiest man or woman in the world if you look for happiness in the right place'.

If you take the time to look around you, I'm sure you can find many things you are grateful for. Think about all the moments that you would miss in your busy day if they weren't there, and some of the little things you take for granted. How can you slow down to appreciate them—to tune in to the positive things in your life? Initially it does take a little extra effort to give gratitude and practise kindness and compassion, but once you practise it more frequently it becomes a habit that is ingrained in your life.

Sometimes people initiate a gratitude practice and enjoy it for a while but then it slowly slips away. I believe practising gratitude should be a daily healthy habit, just like brushing your teeth. Someone I work with, Tony Bongiorno, agrees with me. Tony, who runs a successful, family-owned financial services company providing financial advice to medical professionals, has been practising gratitude daily for about 30 years. He discovered meditation and gratitude practices back in 1992 as part of his recovery from cancer, and he continues to practise it to this day. Over the years he has developed his own practice based on what he has learned, which includes transcendental meditation (TM), visualisation exercises, mindfulness and daily gratitude practices. Tony explains that he does a simple daily gratitude practice for himself every day and writes down three to five things that went well in his day or that he is grateful for personally and professionally. He says that in a busy, stressful workplace it is easy to get caught up in the daily difficulties and challenges, but it is not useful to tune in to that—it is far healthier to focus your attention on the good things happening around you. Not only does Tony recognise the importance of a gratitude practice for himself, but he also shares this attitude passionately with his team in the form of wellbeing programs and training. A happy workforce is an engaged workplace, and an engaged team is a productive one, so everybody gains from being more mindful and grateful.

Getting your daily DOSE of happiness chemicals

I have already briefly mentioned that when we practise gratitude, kindness and compassion our bodies release happiness chemicals. Let's talk about these a bit more.

DOSE stands for dopamine, oxytocin, serotonin and endorphins, a complex concoction of chemicals, hormones, neurotransmitters and physiological responses that occur in the body when they are stimulated.

Dopamine

Dopamine—often called the 'reward' chemical or 'feel good' hormone—is a neurotransmitter that is an important part of the brain's reward system. It is associated with pleasurable sensations, along with learning, memory and a sense of achievement. It enables motivation and gives you the determination to achieve your goals, desires or needs. You get a surge of dopamine when you complete a task that makes you feel good and gives you a sense of accomplishment. Unfortunately, the effects of dopamine are fleeting, and this is why we constantly seek it to give us instant gratification.

Oxytocin

Oxytocin—also known as the 'love hormone'—is essential for childbirth, breastfeeding and parent–child bonding. It is stimulated by physical affection, human touch and intimacy: even just giving someone a hug will produce a surge of oxytocin. It helps promote trust, empathy and connection, and forms strong relationships. Unlike dopamine, which is fleeting, oxytocin has a lasting effect on you and can leave you feeling content, safe and calm for hours.

Serotonin

This hormone and neurotransmitter is often known as the 'mood stabiliser'. It helps you calm down after a stressful event and regulates your emotions. It is also responsible for regulating some of the base bodily functions, such as sleep, digestion, learning ability and memory. One of the best ways to produce serotonin naturally in the body is to get outdoors in natural sunlight, which we all know makes us feel good.

Endorphins

Runners know this one well. Endorphins are released during moderate- to high-intensity exercise, and are known as the 'runners high'. A surge of endorphins can keep you going, especially when you're exceeding your limits. It is a natural pain killer, or reliever, that your body produces in response to stress or discomfort. Endorphins can give you feelings of euphoria. They are also released when you engage in rewarding activities, exercise (group exercise and sports) and have sex.

These chemicals are important for feelings of happiness and wellbeing. Low levels of these chemicals can lead to a variety of symptoms that may cause feelings of anxiety and depression, fatigue or make us generally feel flat. Here are some of the common symptoms you may feel when you are deficient in these four chemicals.

o *Dopamine deficiency*

   • Lacking motivation or enthusiasm

   • Having low energy and fatigue

- Procrastinating
- Lacking mental clarity and focus
- Having mood swings, anxiety and depression

○ *Oxytocin deficiency*

- Feeling lonely or isolated
- Feeling stressed or anxious
- Feeling disconnected from family and friends
- Having trouble sleeping
- Lacking motivation and pleasure

○ *Serotonin deficiency*

- Being low in confidence or self-esteem
- Having anxiety or panic attacks
- Feeling stressed or overwhelmed
- Having mood swings
- Not being able to switch off or calm down

○ *Endorphin deficiency*

- Having low energy and vitality
- Having mood swings, anxiety and depression
- Feeling unmotivated
- Having fatigue and lethargy
- Displaying impulsive or reactive behaviours

How to boost these happiness chemicals naturally

The activities listed in figure 8.1 are fairly easy to include in your life. They can give you that daily DOSE of happiness chemicals and that 'get-up-and-go' feeling. Ask yourself how you can increase your energy and vitality by naturally inducing these mood-boosting chemicals, hormones and neurotransmitters.

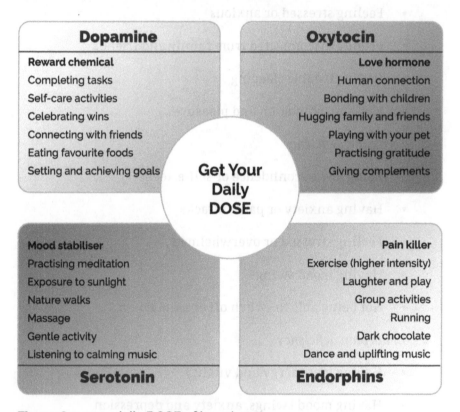

Dopamine

Reward chemical
Completing tasks
Self-care activities
Celebrating wins
Connecting with friends
Eating favourite foods
Setting and achieving goals

Oxytocin

Love hormone
Human connection
Bonding with children
Hugging family and friends
Playing with your pet
Practising gratitude
Giving complements

Get Your Daily DOSE

Mood stabiliser
Practising meditation
Exposure to sunlight
Nature walks
Massage
Gentle activity
Listening to calming music

Serotonin

Pain killer
Exercise (higher intensity)
Laughter and play
Group activities
Running
Dark chocolate
Dance and uplifting music

Endorphins

Figure 8.1 your daily DOSE of happiness

Easy gratitude journalling

One way to practise daily gratitude effectively is by journalling. You can buy some fancy gratitude journals from newsagencies or bookstores and many people like these as they prompt you with quotes and questions to help you write. I personally prefer to keep it as uncomplicated as possible. That way I am more likely to do it.

I simply reflect on three things that went well, or that I am grateful for in my day, and I write them down in my journal/diary. I used to only say them in my mind, but I found that I would usually say the same things over and over, like being grateful for my family, my wife, my children, my health, and so on. However, when I started to write them down I aimed to write something different every day and it helped me search for more small moments in my day to be grateful for. I usually journal at the end of my day or some time before bed so I can go to sleep with a good feeling. Someone once said to me, 'If you want to wake up happy, go to bed grateful.' Try it—it's simple but very effective.

To extend this practice a bit further, make an effort each day to send someone in your life a message to express your gratitude. This is a win–win situation: we feel good for thinking of them and they feel good when they receive your message. So often we want to do more for our family, friends, colleagues and people around us to show we appreciate them, but sometimes life just gets too busy and we forget. Make a point of sending somebody a message to show you appreciate them and make sure you actually do it. It may be useful to create a short list of people you are grateful for in your life and then systematically go through the list and send a few messages per week. The messages could be as simple as a text message, an email, a card, a hand-written letter, a gift, a care package or anything you feel would make their day. Take a moment to think of somebody you'd like to share your gratitude with.

Random acts of kindness

You may have heard this term before. It's a way of taking kindness and compassion to a whole new level. It's where you randomly do something kind for someone in your life and sometimes even for a complete stranger. It could be as simple as leaving a nice note for a colleague, randomly buying the person behind you in the coffee queue their morning coffee or sending a small gift to an old friend. It could even be doing something for the environment, like planting a tree. It's simply doing a good deed for no reason other than to spread more kindness in the world. You can even do a random act of kindness for yourself and spoil yourself with a treat.

Figure 8.2 presents a few unique ideas—but the sky is the limit. You can get as creative as you like with this practice.

Figure 8.2 random acts of kindness

I love this concept. Occasionally I set myself a challenge to practise it by asking myself, 'Who can I surprise today?' or 'Whose day can I make really special?'. I set about sending them a message, a card, a small gift or anything that will make them feel good.

What can you do to share gratitude, compassion and kindness in your world? Who can you surprise today?

Ladakh, Indian Himalaya

A simple act of kindness in a remote area in the Indian Himalaya remains with me because of the immense joy it brought someone. After many days of harsh trekking at altitudes of between 3000 and 6000 metres through some of the most unique scenery I have ever encountered, I was exhausted and needed a wash to rejuvenate my tired body. The surrounding landscape was basically a high-altitude desert with nothing but unusual formations of sand and rock and very little water or greenery, so it was a luxury to find a running mountain stream. I washed in the invigoratingly cold water and as I was drying myself off and putting some moisturising cream on my tired, cracked feet, I noticed some movement in the rocks ahead of me. At first, I thought it was some kind of animal camouflaged by the rocks, but then my eye tuned in to see it was an old lady perched up on the rocks having a rest from carrying her load. She must have been from one of the small mountain villages that I could see nearby.

I finished dressing and walked towards her to say hello. We greeted each other with the traditional Ladakhi gesture, hands clasped in prayer fashion in front of the heart, saying 'Jullay', which is similar to saying 'Namaste' in Nepal or India. 'Jullay' is an uplifting gesture that means many things, such as hello, goodbye, thank you, good fortune and respect, among others. Her beautiful smile cracked through her weather-worn face as she motioned me to sit next to her. Her deep wrinkles spoke a thousand words of decades of hardship in this harsh high-altitude environment. She must have been about 80 years old and I noticed she was carrying a full basket of firewood on her back. I thought to myself she must have travelled quite far as there weren't any trees within immediate eye distance. I offered her some water and sweet biscuits from my pack and we sat together exchanging smiles and eating snacks.

I then had the random thought of offering her some of my moisturising cream to relieve her dry, parched skin. I motioned to her my offering and she smiled with a nod. As I massaged the cream into the deep wrinkles and cracks of her coarse hands, her face lit up with pure joy and gratitude. I was sure this was the first time she had experienced anything like this. It was a special moment that demonstrated the power of touch (releasing oxytocin) and how simple it is to bring immense happiness to somebody through a simple act of kindness. I gave her the rest of the tube and she accepted it gratefully with a gesture of 'Jullay', as she strapped the load of firewood to her back and slung the strap over her forehead.

We walked together up until the nearby village, happy in each other's company without the need to communicate with any words. As she entered the rocky walls of her village, she motioned goodbye with another final 'Jullay' gesture, hand placed in front of her heart, as I continued on my trek. I glanced back for a moment to see her surrounded by the other ladies of the village, who were laughing, smiling and feeling her soft, smooth hands. She lapped up the attention as though she had just brought gold into the village as they touched and smelt her hands. This experience taught me that sometimes the smallest act of gratitude or kindness—even one that seems insignificant to you—can give somebody immeasurable joy and happiness. We were both richer for the experience

When I had completed my final trek through the Himalaya (after many months) I gave away all of my trekking clothes and boots to the local people in a small village. My Scarpa boots and thermal clothes were very well worn and showed obvious signs of wear and tear. However, the Sherpa that I gave my boots to had a smile from ear to ear and the others who received the worn trekking clothes were equally grateful. They accepted my gifts with smiles, hugs and blessings, which sent me on my way with a warm heart.

A gentle reminder

I understand that saying 'thank you' or expressing gratitude may come naturally to many of you, and that unfortunately, sometimes we just get too busy in our fast-moving life to acknowledge this. For example, you might think of somebody and plan to make contact, but life carries you away in its busy-ness again and you forget to reach out. Days, weeks and months pass, and you still don't get in touch. It does take a little bit of extra effort, but the effort is worth it for everyone involved. Gratitude, compassion and kindness are contagious. The more you practise them, the more you will recognise them around you and the better you will feel. Everybody benefits!

I end this chapter with three very simple but effective practices that can help you reduce stress, anxiety and fatigue and replace them with energy, vitality and 'feel-good' chemicals. I invite you to give them a try.

Gratitude and compassion practices

These three simple practices will help bring more gratitude and happiness to your life.

Practice 1: Gratitude journal

Grab a journal, or whatever you prefer, and take the time to reflect at the end of your day by writing down *three things* that you are grateful for, or three things that went well that day. Reflect on both the big things and the small things that happened throughout the course of your day. It's a great practice to end your day or to go to bed with. Remember, if you want to wake up happy, go to bed grateful.

Practice 2: Get your daily DOSE of happiness chemicals

What can you do daily to boost your feel-good hormones, chemicals and neurotransmitters? Take a look at the suggestions below.

How to boost your dopamine naturally	Clear, achievable to-do lists and long-term goals (each time you complete a task you get a hit of dopamine)
	Self-care activities
	Regular meditation
	Exercise, especially with friends
	Eat your favourite foods
	Creativity: writing, music, arts and crafts

How to boost your oxytocin naturally	Any form of physical touch: hugging, intimacy, shaking hands, cuddling kids or pets
	Socialising and connecting with friends and family
	Stroking and cuddling pets
	Getting physical therapies, massage, acupuncture, body work
	Listening to music
	Practising gratitude, giving compliments
How to boost your serotonin naturally	Meditation
	Sunlight exposure: getting outdoors at least 10–20 minutes a day
	Gentle walks or moderate exercise
	Massage
	Listening to calm, gentle music
	Nature immersion
How to boost your endorphins naturally	Higher intensity exercise (group exercise also produces higher endorphins)
	Laughter and play
	Watching comedy or anything that makes you feel good
	Eating dark chocolate
	Dance, movement
	Listening to uplifting music

Practice 3: Random acts of kindness

Make an effort to practise random acts of kindness to people in your life and maybe even to complete strangers. Whose day can you make today?

Some examples are mentioned in this chapter, but it can be anything from leaving a nice note for a colleague, randomly buying the person behind you in the coffee queue their morning coffee or sending a small gift to an old friend. It could be something for yourself, your connections, the community or even the environment. Everybody benefits from these random acts of kindness, so be as creative as you like!

CHAPTER 9

ON BALANCE

This may sound obvious, but finding balance in the various areas of your life will help you improve your overall health and wellbeing, both physically and mentally. Unfortunately, balance is not always easy to attain. When life gets busy with a big project, for example, it can bring you off balance in other areas of your life. You might neglect your wellbeing due to high work demands or other factors that inhibit this balance. When you create time to prioritise yourself and pay attention to your body's needs, your health and wellbeing will be restored, even during challenging periods of your life. This chapter will explore simple ways to reclaim your balance and live more mindfully and intentionally in your life.

Koh Tao, Thailand

After spending about two and a half years cycling, trekking and travelling around the world, mostly in developing countries, I was getting a bit tired of regularly falling sick. I was exhausted and not enjoying travelling anymore. I was also drained from the noise and pollution of the many chaotic cities I had visited, so I decided to take a break and head to Thailand for a rest.

I rented a straw beach hut on a small island called Koh Tao for about $2 a night for a few weeks. I just wanted to lie in a hammock for a while. I shared the hut with a large gecko, who sat on the wall near my bed keeping the bugs under control. I named him Henry and gratefully welcomed him as my mosquito-munching companion given my previous experience with malaria in Africa.

I had never been good at staying still for too long. I had constantly felt the urge to keep moving and I was often on the road or planning my next adventures. However, I had to train my mind to give myself permission to stop and find balance from time to time.

I remember lying in my hammock one day staring out towards the Gulf of Thailand when I came to the realisation that life is all about balance, and I promised myself I would never again feel guilty for slowing down and spending time 'just being still'. This was revolutionary for me. Although I was quite a 'mellow' person (pardon the pun), I also always felt I had so much to do in my life that I couldn't stand still for too long. I learned that balancing out periods of activity with moments of rest is a far more sustainable way to live your life and this has served me well for many years.

I learned that balancing out periods of activity with moments of rest is a far more sustainable way to live your life and this has served me well for many years.

In Koh Tao my days were spent lying in my hammock, scuba diving, island strolling, enjoying the Thai cuisine and lying in my hammock some more. It was just what I needed to balance out the previous year's crazy adventures and to reflect on life. Sometimes, when travelling in countries like Africa, India and Asia, you can be overstimulated by everything you consume and it takes some time afterwards to process it all. For example, in India you can see all extremes of life—death, sickness, colour, hardship, beauty, poverty, beggars, extreme wealth, smiles, laughter and tears—in the course of a few hours.

I remember, while playing frisbee on a beach in Kerala, Southern India, I turned to see a corpse being carried on a wooden crate by mourners. They walked right in front of me, across our frisbee path, to publicly cremate the body. We paused our game to watch a funeral pyre being lit on the beach to send the spirit of the corpse up to the sky. It was fascinating and kind of weird to watch such a moment publicly. Later that night, in reflection, I questioned what I had just witnessed—sometimes it takes time for your mind to process what you have seen.

This also goes for life in general. Sometimes we get so busy that we don't have time to process anything properly, putting us on a perpetual wheel of overwhelming busy-ness, which could trigger cognitive overload and eventually burnout.

I find this is common for high performers I work with who feel this insatiable need to keep moving in overdrive at an unrelenting pace without ever stopping to reflect and process their thoughts. Initially they say that they think if they slow down and meditate or get out of their 'busy mode' they will lose their competitive edge. They feel they have to keep moving at 100 km/h to be on top of everything—to wake up before 5 am to outperform everybody else, and to stay up late to get everything done. They feel that being constantly 'busy' is being productive, but this is not always true. You can be very busy for hours on end but still be unproductive. For example, you could spend two hours working inefficiently in a state of fatigue; or you can spend 45 minutes on focused work after a renewal break and be far more efficient. Don't get me wrong: there's nothing wrong with getting up early and doing your healthy morning rituals, but you should balance this out with earlier nights. It's all about balance.

Back to Thailand: I must admit that after a few weeks of rest and relaxation in my gently swinging hammock, I felt fully energised and was ready to get on the road again. On my last night sleeping in my trusty little straw hut, I heard the 'pitter patter' of little footsteps on the floor underneath my bed. It sounded like a small animal. I assumed it must have been Henry, my gecko companion, but when I looked up to his spot on the wall he was still sitting there, motionless. What could it be? *A rat or a mouse perhaps?* I thought to myself as I drifted off to sleep.

In the morning, while packing my backpack, I heard the same pitter patter of footsteps behind me. I turned around to see the biggest, hairy, black spider I have ever seen running on the floorboards. I can safely say I have never heard footsteps from a spider before! It was definitely time to say goodbye to my little straw hut. Suffice to say I packed my bags with lightning speed as I waved goodbye to Henry, the big, hairy spider and my trusty hammock.

I decided I wanted to take things a little slower than previously, so I started travelling through Thailand, Laos, Cambodia and Vietnam, and along the way I spent most of my time visiting and staying in monasteries to immerse myself in the monastic way of life. I spent a fair bit of time in Luang Prabang in Laos, which at the time was not such a popular tourist destination. It is a small, French-influenced town on the banks of the Mekong River. It is full of Buddhist monasteries and is a training ground for novice monks to spend their early years of monkhood. I exchanged English lessons for learning meditation from the young monks, and Buddhist scriptures from the senior monks. Some days I spent more of my waking hours meditating than doing anything else. This was exactly what I needed at the time, but then, after a few weeks of living in monasteries, I also needed some action. It's all about balance.

Although monastic life is spiritually enriching, you spend long days meditating, resting, meditating, eating, meditating, cleaning, meditating, sleeping, meditating—and the days go on like this. It is a choice that a monk makes to dedicate a life to this way of living and I found it very interesting for a while, but being brought up in the busy Western world, it is not a realistic lifestyle when you have to work, pay bills, provide for your family and generally live as Westerners do. Not that one way of life is better than another, but it is all about the choices we make in life and finding the balance that works for you.

This experience taught me that everything in life is about balance. Life is full of ups and downs, with moments of busy-ness and moments of quietness. There can be stressful times and restful times, times of hardship and times of ease—and ultimately, it is our choice how we balance this out. It taught me never to feel guilty for taking time to rest and renew, especially after busy periods or challenging times, and I learned that this is a more sustainable way of living.

> **We need to invest time and energy in all areas of our life equally to reclaim balance.**

Life lesson: Balance

We can find balance if we give ourselves permission to slow down. After periods of stress or busy-ness, find rest and create space to renew your energy. It's all about balance.

What is balance?

When we talk about balance, most people immediately think of work–life balance, but work is only one spoke in our 'wheel of life' (more on the wheel of life shortly). There are many other factors that bring balance to our lives—for example, relationships, hobbies, personal development, health and fitness, and so on. We need to invest time and energy in all areas of our life equally to reclaim balance.

Try this experiment right now: draw a circle on a page—or just imagine it, if you like—and divide the circle into two sections, as shown in figure 9.1. The two sections are simply 'work' and 'life.' Where do you spend most of your mental energy? For example, if you are at home and you are thinking about work after dinner or in bed, then that goes towards the work section, and vice versa. Now, I do understand that many people today work in a hybrid environment. But think about times out of working hours when you are thinking about work. Those times would go in the work section.

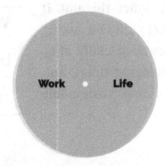

Figure 9.1 work–life balance (or imbalance)

When I ask participants in my workshops how they would split the circle, I'm always surprised to discover that most people write something like 75 per cent work and 25 per cent life, or even 80/20—and it is not unusual to get some 90/10 responses. Certainly, people who love their work automatically find themselves thinking about work much of the time, but it is important to strike a balance. If, for example, you have an 80/20 ratio, only 20 per cent of your time is available for 'life'. When work is given such a big chunk of the circle, something has to be neglected or compromised to make way for this, such as your health and fitness, or time spent with your family, or socialising with friends. When it comes to finding balance and meaning in your life, it's important to invest in the areas of your life that you may be neglecting. This is also true when it comes to resilience: the more balance you have in various areas of your life, the more resilient you are to stress.

If you could turn back time, what would you do differently?

This is a question I often ask the senior executive clients (aged 45–65 years) I coach who work long hours in their high-pressure jobs. Every single one of them says something like:

o   I wish I spent more time with my family.

o   I wish I pursued more personal hobbies and interests.

o   I wish I guarded some of my time to do more things for myself.

o   I wish I was more present with my kids.

o   I wish I looked after my health better.

Not one single person says 'I wish I worked more hours!'

Once you get on that busy high-performance work treadmill and you have filled up your week with a demanding timetable, it's really hard to get off. And the longer you leave getting off, the harder it is. My advice to the under 40s who are working hard to prove themselves on their climb to the top is to guard some time for yourself as soon as you can and invest some of your energy in doing other things in life besides work, even if you love your work.

I was inducting a CEO of a large engineering company into my private coaching sessions and during the first session I asked him what his hobbies and interests were. After some deliberation, he wrote something down. Then I asked him when was the last time he had taken part in that hobby. He stopped and put down his pen. I watched his eyes well up with tears. He covered his face with both hands and started crying. It was a 'penny drop' moment for him. He wiped away his tears and said, 'Oh my God, it's been over 15 years!' He did not realise that he was so consumed by his climb to the top of the corporate ladder that he had forgotten to do things for himself and this is why he was approaching burnout. He did not dislike his job or the company he worked for, but he did acknowledge that everything else was out of balance. He had forgotten about his hobbies, he did not spend much time with his family and he rarely had time to socialise outside of work functions. He is not alone. Many people I meet through my coaching work do not realise how out of balance their life is until it is too late: either they burn out, or their marriage and family life suffer, or they reach some sort of crisis point and then finally seek help.

The good news is, this can all be avoided when we invest our time and energy into reclaiming other areas of our life to find a healthy balance.

How do I know if I'm out of balance?

When things don't feel quite right, you experience more negativity, frustration, anxiety and indecisiveness. Feelings of resentment or guilt are more prevalent and this is a sign that things are out of balance. You might feel you are not heading in the right direction and that you have no time for yourself at all. Physically, your body is trying to tell you that you need more exercise, a better diet and more sleep. But you're not sure how to go about it, so you keep on neglecting these things. You might even start creating some unhealthy habits such as increasing sugar, caffeine or alcohol consumption; smoking; or eating more junk food. You know something's not right but you are caught in a loop that you have difficulty getting out of. This is imbalance.

Balance means something different to everybody and can be based on what you value most in life. Let's say that your most important value is your family. Your children mean the world to you, but you find yourself spending far too much time at work and you cannot spend enough time with them. This is a mismatch of values so you feel frustrated and guilty. You resent work and feel out of balance. Reclaiming balance is about rediscovering, or reprioritising, what is important to you and making time to invest yourself in that. This does not mean giving up your job, but it may mean creating extra time and opportunities to be more present with your children.

A busy entrepreneurial lady named Amanda was referred to me by a psychologist after she experienced a full burnout. Amanda ran a very successful e-commerce business and worked long hours building it up into a multimillion-dollar business. She was mentally and physically burnt out. She had suffered health problems in the past but had not managed them well. The burnout happened progressively for Amanda. Over a period of about eight years she felt exhausted, but her passionate, entrepreneurial spirit just kept pushing through. She had two young children whom she loved dearly, but she barely had time for them. She felt guilty about this, but she was highly driven in her work, so she left the parenting mostly to her husband. She admitted that even when she was with her kids, she was not present, which made her feel even more guilty.

The first question Amanda asked me was, 'How long will it take to recover from this burnout?' I gave her a broad response, saying, 'It could take anywhere from several weeks to a year, or even longer'. I could see that she wanted a quick fix so she could get back to her busy self again. Luckily, after a couple of sessions Amanda changed her mindset towards her recovery and committed to reclaiming balance in other areas of her life. We were both quite surprised that after about eight weeks of self-care practices and doing other things in her life outside of work she had a new zest for life, and she changed her outlook. She spent more time with her lovely children, she pursued a few hobbies, she joined a social tennis club and she slowed down her fast working-life pace. It did take about six months for a full recovery, but it was an absolute pleasure to watch Amanda go from completely burnt out to living a full and abundant life again. Her business was just as successful, but she put other people in place to run most of it while she enjoyed more time for herself and her family.

I have observed this pattern with many entrepreneurs and high achievers who are fixated on their work so much that they forget about everything else in their life. Research by De Mol and colleagues[32] also suggests that this obsessive passion with work can lead to burnout, where people love their work so intensely and are so highly driven to spend all of their time working that they are more prone to burnout. It's great to love your work with a passion but, again, it's all about balance and not overworking yourself at the expense of everything else in your life.

If you are someone who gives themselves permission to slow down, have restful periods and enjoy some time out, then you are more likely to achieve balance in your life and prevent burnout.

Prevention is always better

The good news is, you don't have to wait until you experience burnout before taking some positive steps to find balance in your life. You can take action to prevent it happening in the first place. We've seen in previous chapters that if you spend more time developing your self-awareness and you are proactive in managing stress—along with being more consistent with your self-care practices and adopting the mindfulness techniques we have discussed in this book—you can beat burnout before it happens. Here are some preventative tips to help you find balance in your life.

Tip 1: Come back to 'you' first

Remember, it all starts with *you*: make 'you' and your health a priority first, before anything else. Sometimes we feel it's selfish to take time for ourselves, but the opposite is true. If you take time for yourself to eat well and exercise more, you will be a much better version of yourself for everybody else too. Even if it's a morning walk, going to the gym, a yoga class, taking time for meditation or simply doing something that makes you feel good, make sure you don't feel guilty doing so. Take time to nurture yourself every day and every week. I have one golden rule that I set for myself: the first thing I do every morning is something just for me. It's not for work—no checking emails or doing other work-related tasks—it's just for me. I usually take a morning walk, do some meditation and then eat a healthy breakfast. Three things that are just for me, to nourish my body and mind before I enter my workday. Try it!

Tip 2: Create clear boundaries

The hybrid work model that the world has adopted over the past few years has proven to have pros and cons. For some people it is amazing and they work better from home, while others would prefer to go back into the workplace and be around their team members. One of the main challenges that has arisen out of working from home is creating clear boundaries between your work life and your home life. It is so easy to quickly take the laptop out after dinner and check a few emails, but before you know it you are working right up to your bedtime. Then you might have trouble sleeping because you are thinking about work. It's also easy to be accessible 24/7, checking and responding to emails at all times of the day and night and never switching your mind off. Create some clear boundaries between your work life and your home life.

Tip 3: Schedule 'you' time into your calendar

Unfortunately, in my work I regularly see people who do not balance their work and life. They just keep going hard until they finally collapse. They have their annual holiday, but they fall ill on the first days because they have worked so hard to get to the finish line that their immune system is weak when they finally stop. A better approach is to create balance in your days, weeks and months with mini-rewards and schedule 'you' time into your calendar.

For example, a busy day = a restful night, or a busy week = a restful weekend away, and so on. There is an exercise at the end of this chapter for scheduling 'you' time.

Tip 4: Guard your time

Guard some time for yourself each week. It could be an afternoon off, or just a 45-minute block of time in your calendar. Book some meetings for yourself into your weekly schedule. Use this time to catch up on things that are overwhelming you or to step out of your daily busy-ness and reset. This will make a world of difference to your demanding days and weeks. Also, be mindful of how you organise your daily schedule: try to avoid back-to-back meetings all day long, which only creates more work for you. Ironically, you'll have no time to actually do the work because you're stuck in meetings all day! Create blocks of time for doing your work tasks and blocks for meetings.

Tip 5: Get enough sleep

The foundational pillar of everything is getting a full night of quality sleep. Create an environment that is conducive to this by setting up some healthy sleep routines. Exercise through the day and get as much sunlight as possible. This helps to set up your circadian rhythm (sleep–wake cycle). Close your workday and mindfully unwind for at least two hours before bedtime. Create sleep-association rituals such as dimming the lights, having a hot bath or shower, having a hot drink (e.g. an herbal tea), reading a book and going to bed at around the same time every night. This will help set you up for a good night's rest and quality sleep.

The wheel of life

One of the best ways to reclaim balance in your life is to look at your wheel of life. A balanced wheel of life looks something like figure 9.2.

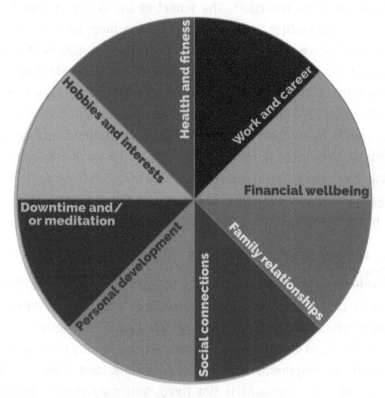

Figure 9.2 a balanced wheel of life

The wheel of life will help you get an overview of where you are spending your time. You may have already done a version of this at various times in your career, but it is always good to revisit it periodically to get a 'bird's eye' view of your current life. It is a simple but powerful tool that helps you visualise all the important areas of your life in one diagram. The wheel helps you to better understand which of your life areas are flourishing and which ones need some attention. You may be surprised by your findings!

This is something I take my coaching clients through to give us a 'helicopter view' of the different domains in their lives and to step back and look at the bigger picture. It is also a great roadmap for setting goals towards the areas you have been neglecting in life and to give you some direction. The wheel of life is a very subjective viewpoint, depending on what you value the most in your life, but it is a good place to start. I often ask my clients to give each area a grading from 1 to 10 (10 being the highest) and to create their own wheel of life. If their wheel is balanced with 7/8s all the way around, the wheel will roll pretty evenly through life, but if it has 9s in one area and 2s in another, the wheel will be unbalanced and not roll very well. Very often there are 8s and 10s in the work area but 2s in social or relationships areas, so obviously we need to do some work in these lower scoring areas. At the end of this chapter you can do this practice yourself using the prompts and questions below.

The wheel of life domains

In an ideal world you have a healthy balance of about eight different domains of life and you invest some time and energy into each domain. The main areas to focus on are health and fitness, work/career, financial wellbeing, social connections, family relationships, personal development, meditation/downtime and hobbies. The naming of these domains is not fixed. You may choose different names or domains—for example, spirituality, religion, professional development and so on—but the main idea is to create a balanced wheel that is devoted to various areas of your life. Here I will discuss eight suggested domains to help you reclaim balance in your wheel of life.

Health and fitness

This is a very important domain as your health and fitness is number one in terms of living a healthy life. When people talk about health and fitness, many of them only refer to the fitness part—that is, the amount of exercise they're doing or the sports they're playing. They don't consider the 'health' part, which is all about your nutrition, rest and sleep, and general wellbeing. All of these aspects are equally important, and we need to take some action towards them to maintain our overall health and fitness. We have talked about the importance of these self-care practices and how to implement them in previous chapters, but ask yourself this honest question right now: 'What can I do to improve my health and fitness?' What's one thing you can start doing today towards being healthier? If you feel you're somebody who already has a good exercise routine, perhaps it's worth looking at getting more rest and restoration. I'm sure you can find something that you could improve to further create balance in your life.

Work and career

This can also be divided into two categories.

The first category is your day-to-day work and how fulfilled you are in your current role, how much you enjoy your daily tasks and how much you like the team you're working with. Think about your motivation and enthusiasm to go to work each day and about the things that energise you and that drain you in your work. Ideally, you'll have more energisers than drainers in your daily workflow.

The second category is the career part (if it's applicable to you). That is, thinking about your career progression. Is what you are doing now in your daily workday pointing you in the right direction for your long-term career? Do you have a clear pathway ahead for the next six months, two years or even five years? Are you taking the right steps towards your future self? Are you growing and developing professionally?

Note: If you are not working, this same approach can be directed towards your studies or daily home life chores.

Financial wellbeing

This may be related to the previous domain of work and career. How is your current financial wellbeing? What value do you place on money and where are you at right now? Do you feel comfortable with your income? Do you feel that you can afford everything that you want in life, or are you struggling to make ends meet? Depending on your financial goals, are you putting some money aside? Are you making smart investments? Are you on track with your objectives? Financial wellbeing means something different for everybody because everybody places a different value on money. But ask yourself right now, *How is it and what could I possibly improve? What does money give me?*

Family relationships

This relates to your immediate family, your partner and/or your children. It could also refer to your brothers, sisters, aunties, uncles, and so on. The main thing to ask yourself here is, are you investing quality time to be with your family, especially if family is high on your priority list? Are you spending time with your kids? Are you connecting with your partner? Are you making an effort to go out and see extended family or have regular get-togethers? Family is often high on most people's values list, but unfortunately, we sometimes get too busy to spend quality time together. Think about it yourself: are you investing time in nurturing your family relationships? Is there anything you can improve?

Social connections

Outside of family, are you making time to connect with friends and socialising? Spending quality time with your friends and meeting new ones is great for your mental health and wellbeing. We are essentially social animals and we need socialisation for our physical, mental, emotional and cognitive development. Without socialisation these areas can decline. Our friends are our support network and it's good to have a friend to lean on in times of need.

The trouble is in our busy lives, we often think about our friends but never have time to catch up. It sometimes takes a bit of extra effort, but it's well worth it. Are you making time for social catch-ups and get-togethers with your friends? Are you surrounding yourself with people who lift you up? Are you connecting with new people from time to time? Sometimes all it takes is a phone call with a friend to lift your spirits up. Is there anything you could do to improve this and stay socially connected?

Personal development

Humans like progress. We like to feel that we are always growing and developing in some way—this can be both personally and professionally. What are you doing to constantly grow, learn and develop your knowledge and skills? Doing this is a great way to realign with things you are interested in and continue to expand your knowledge. For example, it might be to improve your career, or to learn new techniques; or it might be purely for personal interest. Either way, we feel good when we are progressing through life. Whether it's attending courses or workshops, finding a coach or mentor, going to educational seminars or simply reading a new book, see what you can do to continue your personal development. Ask yourself, when was the last time you learned something new and what are you excited to learn more about.

Downtime and/or meditation

I am a huge advocate for this one—it's so important to help you create balance in your life. We're not machines and we're not designed to be 'on' 24 hours a day. It's important to give yourself some time to reflect and unwind. Too often I see people having a break from work by spending time mindlessly scrolling on their smartphones. In my opinion this is not downtime—this is only filling you up with more stress and over-stimulation. Take some time out of your week to practise meditation or simply have some downtime for yourself. What can you do in your day to give your mind a rest? It could be going for a walk, sitting on a park bench, closing your eyes and doing a short meditation practice; or it could be just doing nothing for five minutes. When is the last time you did absolutely nothing? That five-minute break can do you a world of good in an overwhelmingly busy day.

Hobbies and interests

Busy people laugh at me when I say that it's important to spend time immersed in your hobbies or personal interests. However, I do know this after working with hundreds of burnt-out high performers: people who have more personal hobbies and interests are far more resilient towards work-related stress. Hobbies give your mind stimulation outside of work and help you to de-stress. They can also strengthen different regions of the brain. When the wheel of life is dominant in the work/career area, there is usually no time for hobbies or activities that interest you. Think about the things you liked to do when you were younger, or the things you've always wanted to do but just did not have time for. It could be anything from learning a language, playing a musical instrument, playing a social sport, learning art or anything that is of interest to you. Ask yourself what you can do to discover more hobbies and interests and what steps you can take to make them happen.

* * *

All of these simple tips can create a huge shift in your life, once you begin to find more balance among the spokes (domains) in your wheel of life. That way, your wheel can roll more smoothly through life. Take time to do the exercise at the end of this chapter to get the wheel rolling.

Adopting a positive and growth mindset

One other aspect we can add to creating balance in life is adopting a positive and growth mindset. In simple terms, having a positive mindset means that you are optimistic about the world around you, you expect that good things will happen to you and you view the world through a positive lens. In contrast, a negative mindset indicates that you expect bad things to happen and you struggle to view the world positively, or you constantly worry about things going wrong. One of the diagnostic signs of burnout and poor mental health is being cynical or negative about everything and everyone around you, especially when you are feeling fatigued. In reality, some days can be tough and we struggle to see the good in the world around us, but the main challenges in your life can also be your biggest teachers and opportunities for growth.

Some of the biggest challenges in my life have led to a forced change, which has always been for the better and often a blessing in disguise. One particular event comes to mind when the company I was an employee at had a restructure and many of us were forced to quit at very short notice. Although it was difficult at the time, it turned out to be the catalyst for starting my own business, which I am eternally grateful for. Think back over the course of your life where you may have been resistant to change but something happened that made you change. Was it a good thing? When you adopt a positive mindset, you can begin to view the world with a different lens and learn from experiences that happen in your life.

Ways to nurture a positive mindset include:

o focusing on your strengths and positive qualities

o keeping up your self-care

o practising gratitude for the good things around you

- ○ positive self-talk or positive affirmations (e.g. 'I am enough')

- ○ bringing yourself back to the present when the mind wanders off into the past or future

- ○ questioning your negative thoughts and turning towards them

- ○ surrounding yourself with positive people who lift you up (not drag you down)

- ○ setting good intentions to welcome and recognise the positive things in your day.

Similarly, a growth mindset is when we see challenges as an opportunity to grow and learn from a situation. Having a positive and growth mindset does not mean we avoid difficult or unpleasant situations; it is how you approach them and how you can learn from them. A growth mindset versus a fixed mindset will help you be more adaptable to change, willing to try things and learn from them and let go of things that you cannot control. Figure 9.3 summarises the difference between fixed and growth mindsets.

Adopting a positive and growth mindset helps you face challenges in a different way—you can meet difficult situations head on with the intention to learn and grow from the experience. It also helps you to be mindful when you are slipping into negative or fixed mindset patterns and do what you can to change your approach and reframe it positively. All in all, when you adopt a positive and growth mindset approach to how you view the world, everything seems more achievable rather than too difficult. Charles Darwin got it right many years ago when he said, 'It is not the strongest of the species that survives, nor the most intelligent, but rather the one most adaptable to change.'

Figure 9.3 fixed vs growth mindset

I'll say it one more time, *it's all about balance*. What can you do to reclaim balance in your life? Whether it's a big change or a subtle one, you will benefit greatly from adopting some of the tips in this and the previous chapters. Imagine the feeling you get when all of the domains in your wheel of life are in balance and flourishing as you live your life full of passion, energy and vitality without the risk of burnout. Let's do it!

Balance practices

Practice 1: The wheel of life

We've seen that the wheel of life is a great way to get a helicopter view of various areas of your life that are thriving and areas that may need some attention.

Step 1

Use the following wheel of life (see figure 9.4) and the prompting questions in this chapter to give yourself a rating out of 10 for each life area. For example: in 'Health and fitness', if your exercise is irregular and your daily nutrition is inconsistent, you might give yourself a score of 3 or 4 out of 10. You may want to write some bullet points on what improvements you could make to each area of your life.

Do this for each of the areas and be brutally honest with yourself.

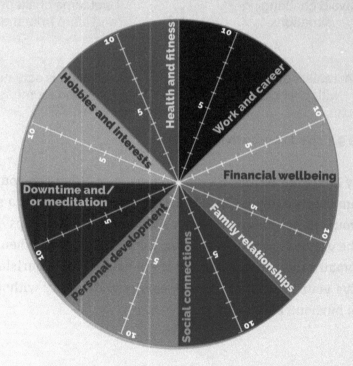

Figure 9.4 add a rating out of 10 for your wheel of life

Step 2

Choose one of the lower scoring areas to focus on and set yourself some personal goals to improve in that area and to bring the wheel back in balance. I always like to set three achievable goals—for example, if it's 'Family', it could be booking in some weekends away with the family, coming home earlier two nights a week to spend time with the kids, and booking in a dinner date with your partner.

Choose your lower scoring area and set three goals to improve this:

1 _____

2 _____

3 _____

You can also choose an area in which you scored above 5—for example, if you gave yourself a 7 out of 10 for 'Health and fitness', ask yourself what you would need to do to give yourself a 10 out of 10. What small improvements can you make to increase this rating? You will find they might be more subtle, like increasing exercise intensity, or reducing certain foods, or perhaps working on your sleep rituals.

This wheel of life is worth revisiting periodically. Continue to make improvements in each area until your wheel is more balanced and you roll smoothly through life. It is normal to have some fluctuations in life depending on priorities—for example, a big project or an important event where that area may dominate for a period of time—but ideally when that event or project is over things should go back to an even balance again.

Practice 2: 'You' time

Schedule 'you' time into your calendar and give yourself some rewards to balance out your busy work. Create your own rewards in the table below.

Examples:

A busy workday = a restful night (no more after-hours work)

A busy, productive week = a restful weekend connecting with family and friends or doing hobbies

A busy month = a weekend away with the family or friends. Go to your happy place—for example, the beach, forest or mountains

A busy few months or completion of a big project = a special reward of some sort; perhaps a mini-break or retreat somewhere special to celebrate and recharge

A busy year = a good overseas holiday or special adventure

Getting through a challenging time = reward yourself with some nurturing—for example, time off, a massage or something that makes you feel good

Activity	Reward
A busy day at work (or home) =	
A busy, productive week =	

Activity	Reward
A busy month of big achievements	=
A busy few months or completion of a project	=
Getting through a challenging time	=

CONCLUSION

Congratulations on reaching the end of the book! This is where your wellness journey begins. I sincerely hope you have initiated some of the mindful practices on the pages of this book and are feeling the benefits already. I hope you will dip back into the book regularly to refresh your memory. Once you adopt your preferred practices as long-term habits, I guarantee you will benefit greatly for the rest of your life.

My hope is that—whether you're feeling burnt out or not—this book has motivated you to seek to live a balanced life for the long term. Too often, I hear people say that they have listened to an inspiring talk, or been to an educational seminar or an amazing workshop, or read a great book that motivated them to make positive changes in their lives. They scribble down some notes, convert the notes into a document and store it safely on their laptop in a file labelled 'Personal Development'. Two weeks pass, and they forget all about it and go back to their old habits again. Please don't let that be you after reading this book. Keep it within reach in your workplace or your home. Write in it. Dog-ear the pages. Make it your own.

I know I've given you a lot to digest, so here is a summary of all the life lessons in one list:

○ *Self-awareness.* This precedes everything. When you develop your self-awareness you become more mindful of your inner and outer environments. You can prevent burnout with awareness by realising what you are experiencing, assessing the situation and taking positive, decisive action in the moment.

○ *Burnout and self-care.* The self-care practices that keep you healthy and balanced are the same ones that lead to burnout when neglected. Through self-awareness and improving your self-care you can be more attuned to your body's needs and more proactive towards your health and wellbeing.

○ *Stress and resilience.* The stress response is only designed for short-term stimulus, which is helpful in a threatening or challenging situation. However, to maintain balance we need to learn to deactivate it when it's not needed and initiate the relaxation response more regularly.

○ *Self-regulation.* The ability to self-regulate gives you the choice to create the space to mindfully choose your response in any given situation rather than simply reacting. Pause, breathe, create space and respond mindfully instead of reactively.

○ *Overwhelm and anxiety.* Remember that *you are not your thoughts.* Overwhelm, worry and anxiety are often created in your mind. Instead of worrying about all of the future 'what if' scenarios that may or may not happen, choose to focus on 'what is' happening in the present moment. Catch stress in the early stages before it manifests to overwhelm and creates further anxiety.

o *Fear and trust.* On the other side of fear there is trust. Turn towards your fear and trust that you will always have the resources you need to get through any situation, no matter how difficult.

o *Purpose and perseverance.* When you align with your purpose and vision you can stay motivated and energised to persevere towards your goals, no matter how challenging life gets.

o *Gratitude and compassion.* Never take things for granted. Focus on being grateful for what you have, not what you don't have. Small acts of kindness, compassion and gratitude can positively change your world, and that of others too. The power of gratitude rests in your ability to positively change the way you view the world.

o *Balance.* We find balance if we give ourselves permission to slow down. After periods of stress or busy-ness, find rest and create space to renew your energy. A happy life is all about balance.

Well there you have it! You have come so far by reading this book and learning the life lessons and practices I write about. Continue your wellness journey by implementing mindfulness in your life using my practical tips to better manage stress, build resilience, stay energised and maintain wellbeing. You have all the tools and resources inside of you. You just need to bring them out when you need them. Continually draw on the techniques and practices from this book as they will serve you well for years to come.

Here's to beating burnout, finding balance and living more meaningfully!

ACKNOWLEDGEMENTS

I never realised how isolating, reflective and transformational writing a book could be, and I wanted to take a quick moment to thank all of the people who supported me during the process.

Firstly, my deepest thanks to Kila and the girls for putting up with me constantly talking about 'the book' and giving me the space to indulge in the many hours of writing it.

A heartfelt thank you to my parents and all of my family (including my in-laws) for believing in me.

A big thank you to all of my clients and contributors who I interviewed while researching burnout and the other concepts in the book. Your unique stories, insights and perspectives are an invaluable part of this book and I'm eternally grateful for your contributions.

Thanks to all who have contributed to this book, knowingly or unknowingly, such as Scott Chapman, John Rowland, Nick Bracks, Tony Bongiorno (and team), Michael Waycott, Margaret Mote, Matt H, Dr Chrys Hensman, Abhay Khot, Karsten Horne, Josh Bronstein, Tess Lloyd, JR, Chris Garnaut, Paul Knapp, Maarten Kila, Nicola Catalano, Hilmar and Svava, Adriarna Nunn, Ben B, Jennifer, and anybody I have missed—you know who you are.

Gratitude to all of my Internal Arts teachers past and present: Master Wong, Chris Milanko, Master Liu Deming, Sifu B Fong and the long lineage of monks, sages and masters that I learned from during my travels.

Thanks to Kelly Irving for her expert guidance and the awesome community in the Expert Authors Academy for their continued support.

Thanks to Lucy, Leigh, Chris, Renee and the whole Wiley team. A big thank you to Sandra, who edited my words and gave them more life.

And a warm thanks to Koda (the dog) and Pepe (the cat) for cuddling up on the sofa with me on those long, lonely writing days.

And finally, a huge thanks to *you* for picking up this book.

Stay in touch at **www.melocalarco.com.**

REFERENCES

1 Goleman, D 1995, *Emotional intelligence: why it can matter more than IQ*, Bantam Books, Inc.

2 Thích Nhất Hạnh (1926–2022) was a Vietnamese Buddhist monk, author, poet and teacher recognised as popularising Buddhism in the Western world.

3 Killingsworth, MA & Gilbert, DT 2010, 'A wandering mind is an unhappy mind', https://pubmed.ncbi.nlm.nih.gov/21071660

4 World Health Organization 2019, https://www.who.int/news/item/28-05-2019-burn-out-an-occupational-phenomenon-international-classification-of-diseases

5 *Forrest Gump* 1994, starring Tom Hanks, Paramount Pictures.

6 World Health Organization 2019, op.cit.

7 2022 ELMO Employee Sentiment Index. The research, commissioned by ELMO Software and conducted by Lonergan Research in accordance with the ISO 20252 standard, surveyed 1016 Australian workers aged 18 years and over between 11 March 2022 and 31 March 2022. The research was conducted through a 14-question online survey. Respondents were members of a permission-based panel geographically disbursed throughout Australia including both capital-city and non–capital city areas.

8   Microsoft 2022. Hybrid work is just work are we doing it wrong?'. https://www.microsoft.com/en-us/worklab/work-trend-index/hybrid-work-is-just-work

9   Digital Resources Australia 2021, https://www.digitalresources.com.au/the-great-resignation-burnout-largest-cause

10 *Gorillas in the Mist* 1988, Warner Bros. Universal Pictures.

11 Seppälä, E 2016, 'Breathing happiness', TEDx Talk, Sacramento. https://youtu.be/Uvli7NBUfY4

12 Bhaskar, S, Hemavathy, D & Prasad S 2016, 'Prevalence of chronic insomnia in adult patients and its correlation with medical comorbidities', *J Family Med Prim Care*, vol. 5, no. 4, pp. 780–84.

13 Hilbert M & López, P 2011, 'The world's technological capacity to store, communicate, and compute information', *Science Express*, vol. 332, issue 6025, pp. 60–5.

14 Frankl, V 1946, *Man's Search for Meaning*, Beacon Press.

15 Anne Lamott is an American novelist and non-fiction writer. She is a political activist, public speaker and writing teacher. Lamott is based in Marin County, California.

16 Hewlett Packard 2005, 'Abuse of technology can reduce UK workers' intelligence: HP calls for more appropriate use of 'always-on' technology to improve productivity'. Rushkoff, D & Dretzin, R 2010, 'Digital nation: life on the virtual frontier', PBS, *Frontline*. Sanbonmatsu, DM, Strayer, DL, Medeiros-Ward, N & Watson, JM 2013, 'Who multi-tasks and why? Multi-Tasking ability, perceived multi-tasking ability, impulsivity, and sensation seeking', *PLoS ONE* vol. 8, no. 1: e54402.

17 Slagter, HA, Lutz, A & Greischar, LL 2007, 'Mental training affects distribution of limited brain resources', *PLoS Biology*, vol. 5, no. 6.

18 Jackson, T, Dawson, R & Wilson, D 2001, 'The cost of email interruption', *Journal of systems and information technology*, vol. 5, no. 1, pp. 81–92.

19 Harris, D 2014, *10% Happier: How I tamed the voice in my head, reduced stress without losing my edge, and found self-help that actually works—a true story*, Hodder & Staughton.

20 Tolle, E 1997, *The Power of Now*, Namaste Publishing, p. 85.

21 Tseng, J & Poppenk, J 2020, 'Brain meta-state transitions demarcate thoughts across task contexts exposing the mental noise of trait neuroticism', *Nature communication*, vol. 11, no. 3480, https://doi.org/10.1038/s41467-020-17255-9

22 Bracks, N 2021, *Move Your Mind: How to build a healthy mindset for life*, Wiley.

23 Tracy, B 2013, *Eat That Frog: get more of the important things done—today!* Hodder Paperbacks.

24 Impostor syndrome, or the impostor phenomenon as it was originally called, was first introduced by Dr Pauline R Clance and Dr Suzanne A Imes in their book, *The impostor phenomenon in high-achieving women: dynamics and therapeutic intervention* (1978).

25 Cathy Freeman, OAM, is a former Australian sprinter who specialised in the 400 metres event, for which she won gold in the 2000 Olympics.

26 Martela, F & Steger, M 2016, 'The three meanings of meaning in life: distinguishing coherence, purpose, and significance', *The Journal of Positive Psychology*, vol. 11, no. 5, pp. 531–45.

27 Catalano, N 2015, *Can't get you out of my head*, Vivid Publishing.

28 Greater Good Science Centre 2018, UC Berkley, https://ggsc.berkeley.edu/images/uploads/GGSC-JTF_White_Paper-Gratitude-FINAL.pdf

29 Kyeong, S, Kim, J, Kim, D et al. 2017, 'Effects of gratitude meditation on neural network functional connectivity and brain-heart coupling', *Scientific Reports*, vol. 7, no. 5058, https://doi.org/10.1038/s41598-017-05520-9

30 Joel Wong, Y, Owen, J, Gabana, NT, Brown, JW, McInnis, S, Toth, P & Gilman, L 2018, 'Does gratitude writing improve the mental health of psychotherapy clients? Evidence from a randomized controlled trial', *Psychotherapy Research*, vol. 28, no. 2, pp. 192–202.

31 Ricard, M, Lutz, A & Davidson, RJ 2014, 'Mind of the meditator', *Scientific American*, vol. 311, no. 5, pp. 38–45.

32 De Mol, E, Pollack, J & Ho, VT 2016, 'Predicting entrepreneurial burnout in a moderated mediated model of job fit', *Journal of Small Business Management*, vol. 56, no. 3, October.

INDEX